AFFirMpress

Michael Sexton has worked as a journalist for more than 30 years in Australia and abroad. He has worked in news, current affairs and documentary. His written work includes biography, environmental science and sport. In 2015 he co-authored *Playing On,* the biography of Neil Sachse published by Affirm Press. *Chappell's Last Stand* is his seventh book.

CHAPPELL'S LAST STAND

BY

MICHAEL SEXTON

AFFiRM
press

Published by Affirm Press in 2017
28 Thistlethwaite Street, South Melbourne, VIC 3205
www.affirmpress.com.au
10 9 8 7 6 5 4 3 2 1

National Library of Australia Cataloguing-in-Publication entry available for
this title at www.nla.gov.au.

Title: Chappell's Last Stand / Michael Sexton, author.
ISBN: 9781925584424 (paperback)

Cover design by Karen Wallis, Taloula Press
Cover Image by Patrick Eagar/Popperfoto/Contributor via Getty Images
Typeset in Granjon 12.75/19.5 pt by J&M Typesetting
Proudly printed in Australia by Griffin Press

The paper this book is printed on is certified against the Forest Stewardship
Council® Standards. Griffin Press holds FSC chain of custody certification
SGS-COC-005088. FSC promotes environmentally responsible, socially
beneficial and economically viable management of the world's forests.

For Neil, Peter and Adrian – the Chappells of Ceduna.
And to the memory of David Mugford.

In the 1970s people were starting to say 'why' instead of 'yes'. It was a reflection of what was happening in wider society. There is an Australian-ism that Jack is as good as his mate, but that never really applied with the Australian cricket administrators and the players. Jack certainly wasn't as good as his mate.

Richie Benaud

IT'S TIME

Ian Chappell's natural instinct is to speak his mind, which is why he was so troubled leaving the nets after South Australia's practice session in the spring of 1975.

As he tucked his pads under his arm and picked up his bat, the rest of the players were already making their way to the change room at the back of the ivy-covered Members Stand. The Sheffield Shield season was beginning that week in Brisbane. Queensland would play New South Wales. Like a slow thaw following winter, cricket's arrival heralded the approach of summer.

Chappell felt compelled to make some sort of speech on the eve of the season. Despite his prowess with words he wasn't much for the 'rah rah' stuff. He believed bowlers bowled and batsmen batted. If they needed motivation from speeches then there might be something wrong. When he spoke it was direct and honest which is why his mind was being tugged in two directions: what he wanted to say to the team that might set the tone for the year, and what he really thought of their chances.

*

Chappell felt great pride in his state and had agreed to captain again despite handing over the national job to his brother Greg. The captaincy of Australia was in far better shape now than when he had been given it, when the side was listing. Bill Lawry was sacked as the 1970–71 Marylebone Cricket Club (MCC) became the first English side to tour without dropping a Test. They also drew plenty, with the seven-match series ending 2–0. Coming off the back of the 1968 series, which ended one-all, Test cricket was drifting into dreariness.

This wasn't new. In the 1950s Sir Donald Bradman worried that Test cricket was going stale. He conspired with Richie Benaud and Frank Worrell to play audaciously during the West Indies' tour of Australia in 1960–61. It produced a summer of adventure, a tied Test, knife-edge results and a concluding street parade through well-mannered Melbourne for the West Indians. The ticker tape that floated down on the visitors carried the thanks of a grateful cricket nation for switching the game from black and white to technicolour.

The colour started fading again as the decade wore on. In 1964 the Ashes were retained, Australia winning one Test from five matches. The next two series both ended one-all. By the time Ian Chappell went out to take the toss for the first time as captain, at the SCG in February 1971, the past 27 Ashes Test matches had produced only nine results, with four going Australia's way.

It wasn't the kind of cricket Chappell had been brought up to play.

Observers might have known things were going to change in Australian cricket when Chappell arrived at Heathrow Airport for the 1972 tour wearing a mauve safari suit. When required, the team wore blazers and ties, but otherwise Chappell's Australians were a paisley and striped-blur with moustaches and sideburns going back and across. They were all flared trousers, flared collars and flared hair. In London they set up camp in the Waldorf Hotel where they drank half pints of double diamond pale ale with Mick Jagger. Before the first Test at Manchester they went en masse for a trim at a hair salon owned by George Best.

It matched a fashion sentiment at home where a seismic social and political shift was at play. After 23 years in power the conservative government faced defeat. Labor leader, Gough Whitlam, promised to sate the mood that it was time for change.

When elected Whitlam tried wresting the country loose from its cultural bondage. He wanted a new national anthem, the end of British honours and knighthoods, to withdraw from America's war in Vietnam and to make tertiary education free. He urged that books, films, music and theatre be written for and about Australia. Not everyone liked it but those who did adored it. It was the anti-cringe or, as Paul Keating would later call it, 'the cultural strut'.

When the Australians took to Lord's for the second Test match in 1972 they were set to strut.

They really shouldn't have been because they were already one down in the series after losing at Old Trafford by 89 runs. Chappell was facing accusations that he was too cavalier. In that first Test, after winning the toss and batting, England posted 249 with lanky debutante Tony Greig top scoring with 57.

The Australian openers were skittish in reply. Keith Stackpole was dropped on consecutive balls. When the second fell to the turf he scrambled through for a single only to see Bruce Francis clip the next one within inches of the grasping fingers of John Snow.

The pair steadied and built the total to 68 when Francis was lbw to Basil D'Oliveira. Chappell arrived at the crease to face Greig who bent his back and reared the first delivery short. Chappell loved to hook and the ball left a sweet red cherry imprint in the middle of the blade. It soared across the pale Manchester sky ... and into the hands of Mike Smith standing at fine leg, his heels touching the boundary and his arms outstretched above his head. In the second innings another mistimed hook shot, this time off Snow, had Chappell caught behind for seven.

Critics suggested that the shot was too risky for a number three because when it failed it exposed the middle and lower orders. Chappell believed he had been playing the shot well and was unlucky. Later he would advise his players that they shouldn't whinge about short bowling because 'you've got a bat in your hand, so use it'.

At Lord's, Chappell and Ray Illingworth had conducted the coin toss in drizzle and the overcast conditions made the match resemble one played on a wet driveway by kids using a tennis ball half wrapped in electrical tape.

The conditions helped debutant Bob Massie to eight English wickets in the first innings. The Australians weren't spared in their first dig. Francis was clean bowled first up by Snow. Stackpole made five. At 2/7 the Chappell brothers were at the crease. England knew what to do and, on a greasy deck under a bruised sky, they launched ball after ball at the Australian captain's nose. He attacked back. The cherries grew as he hooked and pulled. Most fizzed to the boundary – one went over for six. The brothers added 75 until Smith again caught Ian at fine leg, this time running to catch the chance off Snow. Greg finished with 131 and Rod Marsh made 50.

After Massie picked up another eight-wicket haul in England's second innings the tourists needed 81 to win. Stackpole was unbeaten on 57 when he joined the celebrations in the Australian change room. The Australians won with so much time to spare that the ground cleared out and so the planned royal visit scheduled for tea-time had to be abandoned. Instead the team visited Buckingham Palace that evening.

After the third Test was drawn, and England won the fourth with Derek Underwood spinning Australia out on a grassless deck (something of a rarity in Yorkshire), the series moved to London's The Oval for the fifth and final Test. There the Australians threw down a marker, Lillee taking ten wickets and the Chappells both making first innings centuries.

Needing 242 to win, the Australians were 1/116 at stumps on the fifth day with Stackpole and Chappell in command. The next morning Chappell, on 37, swept Underwood. The ball hit the top edge, cannoned off his face and into the grateful hands of Bob Willis. A collapse followed and, at 5/171, the momentum had swung.

The series decider was now a thrilling drama played out on the final day of the final Test. The tension built on every delivery faced by Paul Sheahan and Marsh. Sheahan hadn't had a prolific tour but continued playing off the front foot. As the 71 runs were whittled away Marsh became antsy, wanting the contest finished. He wasn't going to nudge and push runs. Instead, his hammer blows through mid-wicket were exclamation marks on the statement 'We will win'. The sight of the pair running from the pitch, whirling their bats above their heads like windmill blades, broadcast the joy of victory to Australia.

Chappell saw Marsh collapse into 'an untidy heap' in the change room and put it down to the release of tension. Marsh believed part of that tension was the fear of being responsible for a loss and, in doing so, letting down his mates.

Standing amid the celebrations Chappell felt the match was a watershed. He would later reflect that it was the best Test match he ever played in. England was the leading side in the world at that stage and the match could have gone either way. That it went to Australia convinced him and, he believed, others in that squad, that they were good enough to match it with the rest of the world.

As they packed their gear for home no-one felt the joy more than tour manager, Ray Steele. Although a veteran cricket administrator, his sporting grounding came from Australian Rules football. He had played with Richmond in the 1940s, a blue-collar club that was intolerant of pretension.

In 1972 he had watched, with growing admiration, Ian Chappell cope with the demands of being captain, a job he believed meant having to be a guide, philosopher, friend, diplomat and orator.

Chappell was not burdened with older players who may be prone to second-guessing or cynicism. With 38 Tests behind him, the captain was the most experienced player in the squad and, at age 28, he had only three players older than him. Moreover, five players had never played a Test match, and his strike bowler, Dennis Lillee, had played only two.

Cricket, although a team game, can be a singular sport. A century or a bag of wickets can come amid a heavy defeat and the individual is still feted. Steele saw Chappell turn the equation around. His way of describing it was that this was the least 'average-conscious' side he had toured with. Its objectives were team-based and Chappell led them with a 'freedom from humbug'.

One example was early in the tour during a lead-up match against Lancashire in May, when county captain, Jack Bond, took Chappell on a tour of the facilities at Old Trafford. He showed Chappell his own changing room and invited him to share it with him during the match. The 'Captain's Room', he added, would also be available to Chappell during the first Test.

Chappell looked around, remarked how small it was and that while he appreciated the invitation he would decline because he wasn't sure how the rest of the Australian side would fit.

Although Lord's belonged to Massie, Steele identified Chappell's against-the-odds attacking innings as one of rare character or, in football shorthand, 'guts'.

The team was like its captain – decisive, skilful and daring. And they played, he concluded, the sort of cricket the public would pay to see.

*

The first hint the players had of the Australian public's resurgent interest in cricket was when traffic groaned to a standstill in Drummoyne in Sydney's inner west. It was October 1972 and the squad had re-united the evening before for the first time since returning from England. They were in town to play a charity match for the New South Wales Spastic Centre.

Ian Chappell asked the driver how much further they had to travel and was told the ground was still a fair way off. All he could see out of the window was a street choked with cars. Eventually he and the other players decided that the only option was to hoof it. As they walked they melded into a stream of fans carrying eskies and bubbling with enthusiasm.

Chappell was stunned by the numbers and wondered aloud to Marsh why people were coming along to watch this game. When they arrived at the ground it was packed. Veteran cricket writer Ray Robinson estimated the crowd to be 15,000 which he believed was the largest cricket crowd to attend an Australian suburban ground.

This was what the players hadn't realised while they had been away – the impact they had on supporters at home. The Oval Test match was the first time the ABC had broadcast a game from England, and Marsh and Sheahan's exuberance was re-enacted in lounge rooms across the nation.

The Drummoyne crowd was the beginning. Shield cricket was boosted with the 1972 tourists distributed across the states, particularly the non-powerhouse ones. The Oval Test had been the first in which no player from New South Wales featured. Meanwhile six players were from Western Australia, three from South Australia and two from Victoria.

In December the Australians were back playing Test cricket. In the first Test against Pakistan in Adelaide, Chappell thumped 196 and Marsh 118 in the first innings, setting up victory by an innings and 114 runs. Australia took the series 3–0. That is how things tended to roll from then on.

Australia then went to the Caribbean and won 2–0. After the first two Tests of the 1973 series were drawn Chappell lost Lillee and Massie to injury and form respectively, and turned to Max Walker and Jeff 'Bomber' Hammond to bowl in the body-wilting humidity. The line-up produced a remarkable 44-run against-the-odds victory in the third Test in Port of Spain. Australia then won the fourth Test in Georgetown by ten wickets.

The following home summer New Zealand was done 3–1. A

year later England was crushed 4–1, with both Lillee and his new mate, Jeff Thomson, bowling at a terrifying pitch.

Chappell had inherited a team in a time of crisis and rebuilt it into the most exciting side in world cricket. Crowds surged to see Lillee and Thomson hurl down deliveries that turned Marsh into a contortionist behind the stumps. Greg Chappell batted elegantly and Doug Walters with élan.

Handmade signs appeared in the outer, renaming grassed, general admission hills as grandstands in honour of Walters and the Chappells. In the punters view, the Poms had been roasted, and the West Indies, Pakistan and New Zealand dispatched.

In 1975 the Ashes Test series in England was shortened to four Tests to accommodate the first limited-overs World Cup. In that tournament Australia reached the final at Lord's against the West Indies. Played to the soundtrack provided by South London's Caribbean migrant community, the teams forced each other to high peaks of effort. Clive Lloyd's 102 was tempered by Gary Gilmour's 5/48 as the West Indies set Australia 291 off 60 overs.

Early in his innings of 62, while batting with his brother, Ian Chappell pushed a ball to cover where it was misfielded. As he took off for a single, Viv Richards pounced on the ball, turned and threw down the stumps to dismiss Greg. A direct hit from Richards had earlier run out Alan Turner. Soon he would combine with Lloyd to run out Ian Chappell.

The calypso emotion ran high as the Duke of Edinburgh handed the trophy to Lloyd. Chappell then set his side for the Ashes. In the opening match Australia crushed England by an innings and 85 runs. The remaining three Tests were drawn, with one – the third Test at Headingley – unable to be completed after the pitch was damaged as part of a political protest.

As stumps were drawn on the final day of the final Test at The Oval, Chappell confirmed his time as captain was over. His 192 in the match showed he was still a brilliant batsman but he was at the end of his tether with leadership. Ray Robinson, who chronicled every Australian leader from Dave Gregory on, wrote that Chappell placed more pressure on opposing batsmen than any other Australian captain he had seen. The pressure of the job, though, had taken its toll. He would later say that while he enjoyed some of the battles he had with cricket authorities they wore him out in a hurry.

In this final Test in charge he had enforced the follow on and made England strain on every ounce of its bulldog pride to hold out for a draw. He congratulated Greig and sat in the rooms knowing the captaincy now belonged to his younger brother. By resigning when he decided he had had enough, Chappell fulfilled a promise he made to his then wife, Kay, in 1971, when he heard he was replacing the sacked Lawry. He told her he would never let the bastards get him like that, and they hadn't.

Chappell had led Australia 30 times for 15 wins and 5 losses and had never lost a series. It was September 1975 – South Australia's first match was in six weeks.

*

Chappell remained one of the standout batsmen in the Australian team – and would make himself available for national selection against the touring West Indies. If asked by Greg he would help him with the captaincy but otherwise he intended to stay out of his brother's way. However, he wasn't quite finished with leadership – there was a feeling of having some unfinished work to do in Adelaide. In the past his priorities had been to give everything to Australia and then, if there was anything left over, to South Australia. If there was still anything left over after that, Glenelg got it. He announced now that he was devoting his 'time and energies to leading South Australia back as a cricket force'.

This was not going to be easy.

Chappell had enjoyed success as a state captain, winning the Shield title in 1970–71 but things had deteriorated since. The past two seasons had been horrible, with the side only winning one game each year and finishing bottom of the table.

Chappell lay much of the blame on a lack of resources, saying it was 'a joke the way cricketers in South Australia are prepared for first-class cricket'.

Grade pitches were regularly underprepared, as were players. It was opener Ashley Woodcock – a student of physical fitness and science – who arranged a pre-season training camp in the Adelaide Hills for the state squad not the SACA. There were no specialist coaches for juniors and no financial incentives for veterans. It resulted in a mixed squad of experience, kids and unknowns.

Chappell weighed up the group. There were two spinners in their twilight – Terry Jenner and Ashley Mallett. Wayne Prior was quick but green, and all-rounder Gary Cosier had played well since coming from Victoria. Woodcock was a handy opener and there were two promising young batsmen in David Hookes and Rick Darling.

Chappell believed that if all went well South Australia could rise to third place on the table. Not many inspirational speeches have ended with the goal of finishing mid-table. But for some reason he ignored reality and went with hope. As he entered the rooms and called for attention he looked at the team and told them there were some wise old heads that would help the young guys get through tough times. He asked simply for contributions. Not necessarily five-wicket hauls or centuries, but a regular contribution from everyone.

If that happens, he said, 'I believe we can win the Sheffield Shield.'

In making that bold but unlikely prediction Chappell took a stand against the mediocrity that had crept into his state team – but there was more. At a press conference where he announced his retirement as Australian captain a few weeks earlier he was asked if he had any regrets. He took a long draw on his cigar and puffed out a grey cloud before admitting to a few but then adding: 'If you are captain of a team, you have to be seen by your players to be a leader and you've got to stand up for your team and not be pushed around and I think that was part of the success of the Australian side in the 1970s. When I took over in 1972 we realised we weren't going to be pushed around and I think that helped us win some games we wouldn't have otherwise.'

There were things that bugged him about cricket including the pay, conditions, rules, and lack of consultation. He also hated seeing South Australia being pushed around. He was going to take a stand against them all. It was to be his last season – might as well make it one to remember.

CHAPTER ONE

WARMING UP WITH THE WINDIES

Within moments of the plane carrying the West Indies' touring party touching down in October 1975, the side came face to face with Australian cricket royalty. Clive Lloyd descended the stairs and was met by a group of men in suits. Normally access to the apron at Adelaide Airport was restricted to workers wearing white overalls and earmuffs, but this was no ordinary welcoming party.

'G'day Clive, how are you? Phil Ridings,' said the Australian selector, extending his hand in introduction. 'This is Sir Donald Bradman.'

As a brisk wind blew hair and ties askew, one by one the side shook hands with the man who had dominated the sport in Australia since the Depression. His mythical performances with the bat had morphed into captaincy and later into duties as a selector and administrator. Bradman had a hand in picking virtually every Test side since 1936, and he dominated the Australian Board of Control for International Cricket. Although his only official role now was as trustee of the South Australian Cricket Association (SACA), and its board delegate, he retained a status of almost unquestioned genius.

The West Indies team seemed excited at that moment. They would begin their three-month tour playing in South Australia in front of the greatest batsman in history. They were a young group, with Michael Holding, Gordon Greenidge, Viv Richards and Andy Roberts finding their way in the game alongside seasoned players like Lloyd, Roy Fredericks, Deryck Murray, Alvin Kallicharran and Lance Gibbs. As Richards remarked, there were streaks of grey in some of the afros. His own haircut made him resemble the American activist Bobby Seale as he stepped onto the tarmac and shook hands with Bradman.

Richards's brilliant fielding in the World Cup final had made him more notable than his unbeaten 192 in only his third Test innings. That was almost a year earlier in Delhi where the knock set up victory for the West Indies by an innings and 17 runs.

Garry Sobers thought the young Antiguan was essentially an eye player, meaning he would sometimes hit across the line rather than rely on technique. This worked when reflexes and eyes were young but Sobers believed Richards needed to continue learning to become a complete Test batsman.

He wasn't the only one. When he was selected to tour India, Richards spoke with his father, Malcolm, about his expectations.

'He said to me: "I don't care how many runs you score in

India. Whenever you go to Australia that will be the real test." Funny enough, after that tour, we went to Australia and I found out so very quickly [that] some of the matches against the state teams, it was like being involved in a Test match.'

South Australia's opening attack was not entirely a mystery to Richards though; he had faced one of these bowlers before. It was at Montego Bay in February 1973. His growing reputation in the domestic competition saw him selected in a President's XI to play Australia. Coming in at number five he initially had no problem handling Jeff 'Bomber' Hammond. The first ball was sharp and swung away and so he helped it to the boundary as he did three more times.

'It was perhaps the adrenaline flowing. I never really knew how I was going to build an innings or anything like that; it was just raw talent I brought from Antigua to Montego Bay. I think I got out on about the fifth delivery and that taught me a lesson or two.'

Hammond ended the match with 8/127. His Caribbean workload was enormous because after that match in Jamaica, Australia's fast bowling heroes of 1972 were sidelined; Bob Massie's form had deserted him and Dennis Lillee's back had given way.

Hammond shared the new ball with Max Walker for the five Tests and between them they took 39 wickets.

Their twinned heroics reached a peak in the fourth Test at Guyana when they bowled unchanged for an entire session, taking four wickets each and setting up victory. At one stage

Chappell noticed Hammond walking awkwardly back to his mark and feared he was breaking down. When he asked if he needed a rest, the bowler stridently rejected the offer. He wasn't being pig-headed. Truth was that his jockstrap was caught at an awkward angle and, in the humid conditions, was horribly chaffing him at every stride. Hammond feared if he stopped he would never start again. So on and on he bowled.

Soon the demands of running in and bowling hundreds of overs took its toll on Hammond, as it had Lillee. He began feeling severe back pain and had stress fractures in his foot. For three months after the tour he could only hobble.

His back went during the second Shield match of the 1973–74 season. For the rest of that season and all of the next he worked to rehabilitate a displaced vertebra. Almost every night he exercised in a variety of ways to strengthen the muscles around his aching spine.

Now at 25 he returned to first-class cricket. He had been the baby of the 1972 Ashes tour and understood how Chappell was re-inventing cricket to get more people through the gate. It called for fast bowling and insistent batting.

In his absence Lillee had triumphantly returned to the game and his new-ball partner was Jeff Thomson. Walker was reduced to change bowler with all-rounder Gary Gilmour. Hammond needed to show the selectors he was ready again and the West Indies tour match was the perfect chance.

But he was tentative, bowling only at half pace and trying to emulate Massie's style. Although the speed didn't increase, the rhythm and swing did. The ball moved away from the right-handers through the heavy air and off the pitch. It felt good. Chappell gave him an uninterrupted spell of 12 overs during which he gutted the middle order. He had Rowe caught for three, Kallicharran yorked for a duck, and Lloyd caught Prior for 11: 3/12 off 31 balls.

In a second spell (six overs) he collected Roberts to finish with 4/58. Hammond's brilliant return was an early worry for a touring party already concerned about fast bowling. However, while receiving the congratulations of team mates, Hammond could feel his back tightening.

He was so stiff in the second innings while bowling two short spells (four overs each) that he left the playing arena in frustration. Hammond didn't stop at the pickets, going straight through the change rooms, into the car park and away from the ground. When asked why, he explained that it was for private reasons. Word reached SACA officials that the bowler had sought treatment from his own doctor, possibly painkilling injections so he could continue the match.

After the game the SACA doctor examined him and declared he was fit, 'subject to being able to stand up to the stress of bowling'. The imprecise prognosis left the selectors erring on the side of caution – or possibly discipline. They named him 12th man for the first match against New South Wales.

*

For many in the West Indies' touring party, the four-day match against South Australia was their first taste of the game as played Down Under. Among them was opener Gordon Greenidge who, like Richards, made his Test debut in India in 1974.

Greenidge found Australia an extraordinary experience. People were friendly and open and he remembers being 'wined and dined and honoured at every opportunity'.

Greenidge thought he had arrived in a paradise of sunshine and admired the trees and the spires of St Peter's Cathedral surrounding the Adelaide Oval. Richards was also taken by the gentle scale and framing of the ground. Named 12th man for the match, he had set up at the front of the players' room facing square to the wicket. The attendant made sure Richards knew the location of the fridge containing beers and soft drinks for after the day's play.

Such atmospherics were in stark contrast to the West Indies' experience on the field. Richards would later devote a chapter of a biography to the tour which he called 'Fear and Loathing in Australia', while Greenidge described it as 'blood-curdling'.

They had heard about Lillee and Thomson and seen firsthand Walker and Hammond, but no-one had told them anything about the tall South Australian bowler marking out his run. It was Wayne Prior, known as 'Fang'.

Somehow a story reached the West Indies that Prior was a gravedigger by profession. In actual fact he was a casual labourer with the Salisbury Council. He found it hard to find full-time work because of the time needed for cricket, so he earned money digging ditches and working on a road gang. He was country-lean and straightforward in thought and conversation.

Prior grew up in Two Wells, an hour north of Adelaide, amid market gardens, grain farms and horse studs. Football was his main sport and he only filled in for the cricket team when they were short. He taught himself to bowl using a two-piece ball that he found naturally swung away from the right-handers.

'I didn't bowl that much but one day we were short a fast bowler and I thought, "Oh shit, I will do that." I was quick but all over the place. I never put two balls in the one spot. I think a lot of it is in your wrist action as well, more so than anything. So I think throwing as a kid helped to do that. You go to the beach and skid stones across the water that gives you that whipping motion.'

His pace attracted attention and the Salisbury Cricket Club invited him to train. Football had made him strong and had also robbed him of several front teeth. He wore dentures but one Saturday, while body surfing at Goolwa, he lost them in the surf. The next day he had to play without them. His already ferocious appearance now had a touch of Dracula. His Salisbury team mates called him 'Dentures' but it was Terry Jenner who named him 'Fang'.

Prior was picked for the tour game against England in 1974 but took only one wicket. He finished that season as South Australia's second-leading wicket-taker with 23 but they came at an average of almost 32 runs. Still, he was what Chappell liked in a new ball bowler – nasty and no nonsense – and Prior responded to his captain.

'Ian knew how every batsman in Australia played, their weakness and strengths, and he would inform you how to bowl to this bloke or what to do. They were all new to me so I didn't have a clue. He was great.'

'A bloke of his calibre and experience, you would do anything for him. If he wanted me to bowl underarm I would bowl underarm for him. If I was in one spot too long he would say "Nah, it is time to change direction." He would encourage depending on who you were. He encouraged me.'

Roy Fredericks didn't see the end of Prior's first over. The third delivery was a flash of red that he stepped inside to hook. The mistimed shot flew to backward leg where David Hookes, running with hands outstretched, took his first catch in first-class cricket.

Years later Richards can still see the pace of Prior's delivery and to describe it he just closes his eyes and says 'Whoooo'.

'We always thought Roy was a good hooker, an individual who would take anyone on and was pretty positive about what he wanted to get done. Wow, he went to hook and he hardly got through the shot and we thought this is going to be a very tough series.'

Later the West Indians saw their other opener, Leonard Baichan, wounded by the pace as a delivery from Prior hit him in the nuts. The batsman fell to the ground and was surrounded by South Australian players. Richards thought it looked as if Baichan hadn't fallen over, but rather had been knocked over as though 'shot by a .303 bullet'.

Baichan eventually got to his feet and gingerly stepped back into the crease to face up. The next ball hit him in the exact same spot.

'For some reason, whenever you're watching cricket and you are not behind the bowler's arm, and you're watching from sideways, that ball seems like it's going ten times as quick. It did send a few scares up some of our batsmen's spines who were watching,' recalls Richards.

'The next guy, who at that time was one of the young batsmen, looked at me and went, "We haven't faced Jeff Thomson yet and we see this guy and what he is doing with sheer pace."'

Over the next weeks and months Clive Lloyd's side would lose the Test series 5–1. Chappell believes Australia were not a 5–1 better side than the West Indies but that they knew who they were whereas the visitors did not.

For Richards the fear came from facing hostile, sustained fast bowling, while the loathing came from comments made by some players and many spectators. He found the naked hostility difficult to counter and it eventually overwhelmed him. He called it the hardest and meanest tour he was ever involved in and one that changed his whole concept of Test cricket. Players were beaten before they even left the change rooms.

'I don't want to get direct with some of the names but I think some of the Australian teams went a little bit too far. They couldn't lace the boots of some of these guys and yet the stuff coming out of their mouths ...'

The West Indians battled the popular perception of the

calypso cricketer. The caricature was of the happy-go-lucky player who takes the field as if playing a match on a stretch of white beach sand – cavalier and careless. Richards was sensitive to racism and found it hard to continue brushing off comments and taunts because, 'When you are black you never really know what is inside another man's heart.'

When the disastrous tour ended, Richards and Lloyd sat in a bar in Sydney and promised each other it wouldn't happen again. At that time the pair couldn't have known that the furnace of 1975–76 would be their making. Richards adopted a tougher approach to become the dominant batsman of the next decade. Lloyd began looking for the bowlers to help Roberts fight fire with fire. They needed players who understood how hard it was to dismiss an Australian batsman and how you earned every run against their bowlers.

Chappell's view is that Lloyd was a father figure who cared for his team, especially when they needed support, but that the experience of the tour changed some players. When he next faced the West Indies they were much harder and he believes that came from Richards, Roberts and Murray.

'They gave them the attitude to go with their skills. You have to be hard to win cricket matches and to win them over a long period of time you have to be hard-nosed.'

Both Lloyd and Richards studied Chappell closely and felt there was an aura about him. Just being on the field at the same time gave them a thrill. They admired that he was upfront and direct. They said good morning to him on match day and heard his colourful, intimidatory reply questioning what was so good about it.

Richards recognised a positive streak amid the gruffness. Everything was about the next wicket or the next run. They also knew he set boundaries – it wasn't 'anything goes'.

'You could never accuse Ian of any derogatory remarks about people's race or colour or anything like that – let me tell you that clearly. Ian was just always pretty direct and I will clear him in a second,' said Richards.

'He is always someone I have looked up to but that intimidating factor … some people can't cope with that.'

*

The venom of Fang gave Chappell a weapon South Australia had lacked, but his success was countered by the loss of Hammond.

In the first innings of South Australia's match against the West Indies the two bowlers took seven wickets. In the second innings Prior took only one wicket while Jenner and Ashley Mallett collected eight scalps between them as the wicket lost its pace and bounce.

Although Lloyd was irritated Chappell hadn't given his side more time to bat, after the game he eased himself into a chair in the visitor's change room alongside Bernard Julian and Keith Boyce. Chappell arrived, poured them a drink and joined them to talk cricket. It was part of the game he loved and he made it a team ritual. This is where the game's lore was learnt and no-one absorbed and shared it more than Chappell. It was also a time of building camaraderie by easing hurts and reliving moments.

As part of his 12th man duties, Richards made sure the players were catered to before joining the conversation. He relished this Australian tradition and in years to come was saddened as it faded under Kim Hughes and Allan Border. To him, coming in to see the other team, especially after a loss, was a sign of strength.

'You can be tough on the field but at the end of the day you can be a man and say, "Well done."'

For Lloyd this moment reinforced a basis of success beyond what happened on the field – this was part of team building. It was the strongest impression that Chappell made on Lloyd: that his players were in awe of him.

Although the match had fizzled out to a draw – after dismissing the West Indies for 221, South Australia replied with 369 before the West Indies put on 347 in their second dig – it generated within South Australian cricket circles an excitement not seen for years.

Alan 'Sheffield' Shiell was a first-class cricketer who had moved from the field into the press box where he worked for Rupert Murdoch's afternoon tabloid the *News*. He saw the state side coming together. He liked Woodcock and Rick Drewer as openers and Hookes coming in at six. Past the speed and spin bowling and solid batting, what Shiell sensed most was that the side was more close-knit than in the past. A belief was growing. And nowhere was it growing more than in Gary Cosier.

CHAPTER TWO

UPSET IN ADELAIDE

South Australia v. New South Wales,
Adelaide, November 7–10, 1975

That Ian Chappell was going to make headlines in 1975–76 – mostly negative ones – was never in question, nor was it going to bother him. He believed in action. Most disputes could be sorted out off the field if the parties were willing to talk but on the field he had a limited cricket life to live. If things weren't going well then action was taken. That he would make so many headlines in South Australia's opening Sheffield Shield match against New South Wales, however, was impressive – even by Chappell's standards.

As South Australians woke on Saturday November 8 and collected the *Advertiser* from their front lawns they came face to face with Chappell's arse. On the front page the paper splashed photos of the captain and Gary Cosier with their strides down. They were adjusting their protective equipment and hadn't bothered calling for the fielders to form a modesty guard around them.

One of those who saw the paper was my Grade Five teacher at Westbourne Park Primary School. She held it up in front of the class on Monday morning. Each day we started with 'talks' where some kid had to stand up in front of everyone, generally look at their toes and mumble about something for a few minutes. Among the few highlights of this segment was a demonstration of how to field a cricket ball and the workings of a Hercules transport plane as demonstrated by an Airfix model.

This talk, though, was dominated by the paper.

'Let me show you this and make one thing clear,' she started, her glasses all but fogging up with the intensity of her speech.

'A gentleman never – I repeat, *never* – lowers his trousers while playing cricket.'

When we played the game on the sweltering asphalt playground at recess and lunch we used a tennis ball and bat and vied to be Ian Chappell. He was the undisputed king of Australian cricket. Furthermore, there was a rumour his grandfather had lived a few streets from the school.

When his bum was on the front page, and our teacher was irate about it, we liked him even more. When she glared at us for a response the room broke out in snickers. One kid clapped his hands below the desk. It seemed the joke was on her. Because of our perceived knowledge of the mysterious craft of the game we knew he wasn't 'cracking a brown eye', he was getting comfortable during another heroic knock.

It was a chanceless 86. After winning the toss and batting, Chappell anchored two partnerships with opener Rick Drewer (68) and Cosier (76). The innings was declared 20 minutes before stumps at 8/325.

New South Wales responded with 6/357. Their captain Doug Walters indicated his side would bat on the third day in hope of a lead beyond 100 and in so doing push the possibility of an outright win by South Australia out of reach.

That lit a fuse.

*

Walters appeared to be an anachronism in 1970s Australian cricket. If the with-it Marsh, Lillee and Chappell brothers seemed like the imaginings of Andy Warhol, then Walters looked like a creation of Alex Gurney. Gurney's best-known work was the comic strip *Bluey and Curley* about two larrikin diggers who drank, gambled and wise-cracked their way through the Second World War. Along the way they thumbed their nose at authority and big-headedness while being fearless and dedicated in battle.

Walters had lost two years of cricket to national service but when he returned from the army in 1968–69, and padded up against the West Indies in Sydney, he became the first batsman in history to score a century and a double century in a Test match.

He already had a Test career behind him as a teenager, having scored a century on debut against England in 1965. The sport had been the family recreation in between working a dairy farm at Dungog in the New South Wales Hunter Valley. At 17 he was picked for his state and two years later came into the Test XI.

His explanation of his astonishing rise was that 'the breaks went my way'.

When Walters arrived in the national side he replaced Chappell as the most recent batting recruit. They formed an enduring mateship built on lines not dissimilar to Bluey and Curley. They were usually the last to leave the bar. Walters had a droll sense of humour and his behaviour in the change rooms, whatever the circumstances, became an antidote to the emotions the game brewed. He smoked and played cards before and after batting. A hundred or a duck elicited the same phlegmatic response. Lillee says he never saw him throw a bat or heard him speak ill of anyone.

One moment of excitement that could have been unleashed came at the WACA in 1974 after Walters hooked Bob Willis for six off the final ball of the day to complete a hundred in a session. Chappell watched the moment from the exhilarated change rooms and immediately ordered everyone to hide in the showers so as to leave any celebration the batsman might anticipate in the vacuum of an empty room. The gag fell flat as Walters arrived, dropped his bat, peeled off his gloves and lit a fag before looking for the beer fridge as if not even noting he was alone.

Within the predictable behaviour there was unpredictability in his batting. Crowds grew both anxious and excited when he came to the crease knowing they could see a brilliant innings or a duck. He was also a good fielder and a change bowler who often claimed a wicket when needed. This is why when asked about his mate's form Chappell replied that Walters won Test matches and 'there are not too many cricketers you can say that about'.

When Chappell became Australian captain, Walters knew things were going to change and that they would be playing 'brighter cricket'.

'We expected Ian would go for more results than we had before and that is exactly what he did and we became very successful.'

As skipper, Chappell curbed his late night drinking. He enjoyed both drinking after a day's play and sleeping for eight hours. He found the two acts mutually inclusive. Without a few beers he would toss and turn in bed worrying about facing John Snow or Andy Roberts. With them, his eight hours began the second his head hit the pillow. It was financed in part by the allowance he qualified for as captain. He considered this to be 'dirty money' and put it on the bar every night, disallowing anyone to shout until it was used.

He didn't impose curfews because to him they were – and are – illogical. He believes that the existence of selectors means there is no need for a curfew. Every man who plays for Australia knows that if he does something the night before a match which buggers him up the next day then he is putting himself in danger of being dropped. In Chappell's view that is the greatest curfew that can be imposed.

His plan was to put his glass on the bar at eleven o'clock and announce he was going to bed, presuming the others would take the hint. Walters saw this as a challenge and after several early morning knocks on his hotel door, Chappell had to announce to a team meeting that while his door was always open to the players he drew the line at 3am.

As the team evolved over the years, Walters was the one constant for Chappell. This is why the captain found it so hard dropping him for the fifth Test at the Oval in 1972. Walters's form had been poor in the Tests and he believed he should have been dropped earlier but for Chappell's loyalty. He accepted the news with understanding and urged the team on to victory. It was a gesture and attitude Chappell never forgot and he felt the side won, in part, due to Walters's good grace. As Marsh and Sheahan raced excitedly off the ground after hitting the winning runs, the victory was celebrated with gusto by Walters who had watched the day's play from the bar with Keith Miller.

*

The side Walters led against South Australia in their opening Shield fixture of 1975–76 wasn't the finest XI New South Wales ever fielded but it still contained nine former or future Test players. There was a piece of sarcasm shared in the South Australian rooms that when players were given their baggy blue cap for the first time in Sydney they were also given, to save time later on, a second paper bag containing a baggy green cap.

That the most populous state did well in the state competition shouldn't be a surprise but when New South Wales peeled off 14 title wins in the 20 years after the war (including nine on end at one stage) concerns grew that it wasn't healthy for the domestic game. Shield games were mostly won by teams winning the toss, batting and building enormous first innings totals, then forcing the opposition to try to match the pile. As the wicket deteriorated the second team tended to fall short giving away two first-innings points in a dreary draw.

In 1970–71 changes were made to try to spice up the matches. First innings points were abandoned and replaced with bonus points for batting and bowling, plus ten points for a win.

A batting bonus point was awarded every 25 runs after the score reached 150, and a bowling point was awarded for every second wicket. This meant there was always something for both sides to play for during the match. A losing side could still score bonus points and it made captains, players and spectators think about the game more closely.

The changes worked with games becoming more intriguing and results more regular. Players went out hard early – batting with the sound of the clock ticking in their ears rather than with the feeling they had an age to build a timeless innings. The pressure of the games lifted the standard of Australian cricket, with players describing Shield games as like four-day Test matches.

It was made for a captain like Chappell and he loved the changes – except for one.

There was a rule that the bonus points for batting and bowling would only be awarded during the 65 overs of the first ball. The logic was to effectively force a declaration at that point and keep the game moving.

Chappell was happy to declare after 65 overs but thought the rule disadvantaged the team that batted first. He felt the administrators wanted the captain to declare at the end of the overs but didn't give him any protection by limiting the overs the team batting second could use. Because there were no bonus points in the second innings, a captain might decide to build a large lead and push the chance of an outright win away from the team that batted first. This is the scenario that loomed halfway through the match between South Australia and New South Wales.

South Australia declared its first innings at 8/325 after 63.7 overs (at this time, there were eight-ball overs). At this score the home side couldn't earn any more batting points but the visitors could get one more bowling point, and so Chappell called them in. New South Wales spent the second day batting freely.

After 65 overs they were 4/300 but batted on. This didn't bother Chappell because the visitors were still 25 behind and they had to bat last. At stumps New South Wales had a 32-run lead with four wickets in hand.

At the end of the bonus-point period, South Australia had nine points (seven batting and two bowling) while New South

Wales had ten points (six batting and four bowling). The only thing up for grabs now was the ten points for an outright win and so Chappell expected Walters would declare overnight.

This scenario was likely discussed as the players drank in the rooms on Saturday evening. Through a mist of smoke, Gary Cosier saw the two captains together and heard Chappell tell his old mate Walters that if he didn't declare it could be very embarrassing the next day.

'Ian was very strong on making a game of things,' said Cosier.

'If he sat back smoking a cigar saying "If you do this then I will do that" then it was going to happen. Knowing Doug, he may have done [what he did] only to give Ian the shits and had nothing to do with the game.'

The next morning the two captains were guests on a Sunday morning sports show on Channel 7. Walters and Chappell joined the *Advertiser* sports reporter Gordon Schwartz and former South Australian captain Les Favell in a discussion about the match. Walters was asked if he was going to declare and he replied he wasn't. Chappell sat silently steaming. As they left the North Adelaide studios, Chappell offered Walters a lift to the ground. Once inside the car he let loose on his old mate.

'I said, "Are you fair dinkum, you little prick?" And he says, "What are you talking about?" I said, "Are you going to bat on?" He said, "Yes." I said, "Well I don't know yet what I am going to do but I am going to fucking do something."

'It was a pretty silent drive the rest of the way.'

Sitting in the rooms later, Chappell formed a plan. The second ball was still reasonably new and so he asked Wayne Prior to bowl a bouncer with every delivery 'until I tell you to stop or the umpire speaks to you – if that happens then you refer him no me'.

Prior agreed but on the way out Chappell questioned himself. He thought that if he was going to make a protest then he was the one who should lead it rather than getting someone else to do it. As they went onto the field Terry Jenner told the wicketkeeper, Dennis Yagmich, to be ready for anything because 'Ian is getting shirty with Doug'.

The plan began and a short one from Prior caught Steve Rixon's glove and he was caught behind for six. At the end of the over Chappell called for the ball and told Yagmich to stand about ten yards behind the stumps. He then began lobbing full tosses into Yagmich's gloves.

'I am bowling these things over the batsman's head and hoping it will alert the dopey officials that I am pissed off and then they might come and ask me why I am pissed off. I didn't realise how bloody hard it is – especially when you are a leg-spinner trying to bowl medium pace. [Kerry] 'Skull' O'Keeffe was batting and glaring at me because he thought I was trying to beam him.'

The square-leg umpire, Max O'Connell, was trying to gain the attention of his colleague Robin Bailhache to start calling wides because some of Chappell's deliveries barely cleared Skull's skull.

It was typical Chappell – taking action where words had failed. He had raised his concerns with other state captains and twice had brought it up during meetings with the Australian

Cricket Board. He argued for a system along the lines of English county cricket where an overs limit is placed on batting sides.

Chappell's first over was a maiden and barely had he returned to first slip when he was slapping Prior on the back after he skittled David Colley for one. Chappell smirked to himself that what had started as a protest had turned into a good tactic.

He bowled another over of protest. The tension with the opposition and umpires grew with every delivery that arced through the sky. Adelaide Oval members grumbled and hooted. Chappell's protest was making its point and, in doing so, was winding the game up to a high level of intensity.

It seemed that Prior absorbed it all and continued unleashing it on the New South Wales tail. Len Pascoe was clean bowled for two. Walters had seen enough, calling his side in at 9/372 off 82.5 overs. The extraordinary scuffle had lasted 5.5 overs and returned 3/15. New South Wales led by 47; only about half of what Walters had wanted.

As each grenade lobbed over the exasperated O'Keeffe's head, the rancour between the teams grew. The established order was breaking down. In the visitors' rooms the incredulity at the scene grew into anger. What the hell is he doing out there? Repercussions were to come, and at the end of it Cosier felt the game was probably more ferocious than any Test match he subsequently played in.

*

Although his first-class career was just blossoming, Cosier had already been tutored by two Australian captains. He came up through the grades at the Northcote Club in Melbourne's inner north. He was a child prodigy, starting with the fourth-grade side as an 11-year-old and opening the batting in first grade five years later. His opening partner was Bill 'Phanto' Lawry.

Cosier was a stocky kid known for his flourish of ginger hair, a minimal backswing that provided great power and a jerky run-in to bowl medium-pace sliders. Northcote was a powerful club and he was part of sides that won back-to-back premierships in the early 1970s. When they opened the innings together Lawry and Cosier represented the history and future of Victorian cricket.

Lawry was often characterised as a dour batsman and captain. When he was replaced by Chappell as captain of Australia it was a cultural shift in the expression of how the game was played. Their differences began in the fifth Test against the West Indies in Sydney in 1969. Chappell had replaced Barry Jarman as vice-captain and, in his first Test in the role, Lawry sought him out at a drinks break on the third day.

Australia had made 619 and the tourists were struggling in reply at 8/257. At drinks, Lawry asked Chappell what he made of the situation. Chappell said they should quickly get the two wickets and put the West Indies back in. Lawry shook his head and said he planned to bat again, push the lead over 900 and give them a day and a half of fruitless pursuit. Chappell told him there wasn't much point asking for his advice again and Lawry never did.

'I thought Bill was a pretty good captain in lots of ways but I always thought Bill tried to get himself into a position where he couldn't lose and then he started to try to win. To me that was a crap way of playing cricket. It certainly wasn't the way I was brought up.

'I had the same approach at South Australia. We have eight games, so if we are in with a chance of winning all eight outright then we might win five, which will get us the Sheffield Shield. The other three don't matter.'

Although they disagreed with each other there was never any animosity between the pair. When he became captain Chappell wanted Lawry to continue opening the batting for Australia but he was never selected again.

In 1970s cricket Lawry seemed a figure of the 1960s. Chappell drank and swore and saw the game on its vast scale while Lawry was teetotal and struggled with the wider meaning of something he played for recreation.

'Beer and lemonade and all that,' is how Cosier sums it up. However, he believes such a summary is lazy.

'People who didn't know them would say they were streets apart but I don't think they were at all. They were both unbelievably focused at their trade. Whenever Phanto [Bill Lawry] came back to play at Northcote he would get 100 or 200. It was ridiculous what he did to really good opposition. He treated them like a Test match. He was magnificent. Ian was so hard in his approach and focused and it was exactly the same with Bill.

'I batted a lot with Ian in 1975–76 and he was fantastic on the ground. He had real steel. He would calculate everything, take on the opposition and lead by example. Phanto would do his own thing by keeping on batting and batting.'

Batting with Lawry in a winning club side brought Cosier under the eye of Victorian selectors and he debuted, aged 17, in 1971–72. He looked promising in two games but over the next two seasons his trajectory flattened and then fell. Ian Redpath, Paul Sheahan and Keith Stackpole occupied the top of the Victorian order and Cosier's form at grade level wasn't convincing the selectors of a need for new blood.

Now aged 21 he needed a change and accepted an offer to play at Prospect in the Adelaide grade competition. In his first run he picked up three wickets and few dozen runs and was picked at number three for a one-day game against Western Australia. He had never been to Perth before and came up against two growling moustaches – one behind the stumps and the other hurling thunderbolts at him. It was a revelation in how the game was played.

He was caught Marsh, bowled Lillee for six.

Western Australia cruised to victory and Cosier bowled six overs for no wicket. It was a lukewarm debut but Cosier heard later that Marsh told Chappell that the new kid was the hardest of the bowlers to hit. He believed that may have helped him get selected for the next Shield game.

At state training he watched Chappell batting in the nets. The young players were rarely given advice from the older players unless they asked for it. The presumption was that if they were good enough to be selected then they shouldn't need to have their hand held.

Cosier was drawn to Chappell's technique. He played a little side on and a little open at the front and he moved back and across from leg stump. Cosier was essentially an off-side player who batted side on. So he began mimicking Chappell's style, opening himself more. He found when he moved back it gave him time to have a look first before playing a stroke.

Suddenly the field opened up and he was playing the ball on both sides of the wicket. The runs started flowing. He accepted his role was no longer as an opener but as a middle-order batsman. Under the 65 over bonus-points rule, the first innings was often played like a one-day game. If the openers got a start, and Chappell made runs, then Cosier's role was to come in with about 15 or 20 overs left and take the long handle to the attack.

This is why he relished the opening match against the West Indies in 1975–76, because it offered the chance to build more of an innings. As Cosier waited to bat he looked on at Andy Roberts and in particular Michael Holding with his loping, athletic run-in to bowl. Terry Jenner sat down next to him and asked if he could offer a hint as to how to play Holding.

'He said, "Watch him at the start of his run and then put your head down, tap your bat, or do whatever you want to do, but don't pick him up again until he is about eight steps away." That way you don't waste time and concentration watching him run all the way.'

It was a masterful piece of advice. When he went to the crease it was Holding he faced first and Cosier followed Jenner's plan. He watched him turn and start striding toward the wicket. Head down. Tap. Tap. Tap. Tap. Head up. A few paces. *Bang.*

It worked against Roberts too. By stumps on day two he had matched his highest first-class score of 81 and the next day his batting was so masterful (he shared a sixth-wicket partnership of 138 with David Hookes) that Chappell decided not to declare so as to give his young players more confidence-building time in the middle.

When he reached 96, the West Indies took the new ball, which Clive Lloyd tossed to Roberts. The first delivery slashed through at head height and Cosier played the second one benignly. The next two deliveries he rocked back and cut for two, bringing up his maiden century. When Bernard Julian finally slipped one through to clean bowl him, Cosier had made 130 and was being talked about as a replacement for Ross Edwards in the Test team.

His 76 in the first innings against New South Wales was confirmation of his form. But whatever individual markers he had thrown down in the match, he was now absorbed in a fiery contest ignited by his captain lobbing full tosses.

The opening stand by Drewer and Woodcock knocked off the 47-run lead, but along the way they were so consistently bounced by Gilmour that umpire Max O'Connell warned him to back off.

It was the beginning of a test of wills that remains vivid in the memory of Cosier.

'There was so much aggressive bowling in that game. Colley, who didn't mind bowling short, bowled six bouncers to Mallett and hit him on the hand a few times. I got hit between the eyes by Pascoe and just in the good part so I didn't feel it but had stitch marks down my forehead. Lenny is swearing his head off waiting for me to go down but I didn't feel anything. It just went back and forwards. Colley bounced the hell out of our tail and we bounced the hell out of theirs.'

Pascoe was a bowler that Chappell felt he could disrupt verbally. He would follow him back part of the way to his mark having private conversations that seemed to unsettle the paceman. The result was often that the bowler lost discipline in his rage to punish the batsman.

'Lenny was a great bowler,' says Cosier, 'but if he spent three overs bowling short shit then it was Christmas for Ian.'

Chappell drove and hooked mightily, relishing the match conditions. If South Australia was going to win they needed to build a defendable score quickly. This was Chappell batting for your life, hitting the gaps, running hard and demanding his partners keep up. Anything short was hooked, anything loose was driven and anything wide was slashed.

To his teeth-grinding chagrin, he was on 97 when a ball from Pascoe outside off-stump found an edge and floated into the safe hands of Walters at second slip. At this stage the captain had steered South Australia to 2/205.

The collapse that followed was the first sign of South Australia returning to the bad old days.

Woodcock had made 82 when Pascoe bowled him. A sharp wrong 'un from O'Keeffe had Cosier bowled for 18 and, after scratching around against the growing menace of the spinners, Hookes offered the only further resistance with 35. When Jenner was caught at deep mid-on off O'Keeffe to end the day's play they had lost 5/84. Early on the final day the side was dismissed for 311 – leaving New South Wales almost all day to make 264.

The fourth-day wicket was becoming a spinner's track so Mallett came on early. New South Wales batted with no urgency. At lunch they were 1/53. The afternoon session was equally lazy. Ross Collins spent 50 minutes collecting nine runs before he edged one of Mallett's door-openers to Chappell at first slip. That brought Walters to the crease at 2/70.

Prior dug a ball in that reared up. Walters swivelled to hook it but changed his mind and came inside the line. His boot sprigs caught in the pitch and he immediately felt pain in his knee so vivid he thought he had somehow impaled himself on a stump. He toppled backwards onto the stumps. Chappell's joy at the dismissal turned to concern as Walters clutched at his knee. In the flashing moment he had dislocated his kneecap.

Two players ran to the change rooms seeking help as a ground announcement called for a doctor. The South Australian physiotherapist knelt down and manipulated the kneecap back into position. The injury meant Walters was out of the side for the first Test against the West Indies.

When Walters was gently put onto a stretcher and taken from the field the score was 3/83. McCosker's plodding 34 in almost two and a half hours ended with another Mallett-to-Chappell ball. The momentum was swinging. The home side had taken 3/21 and, at 4/91, New South Wales needed a big innings from someone. And they got it.

Gilmour strode to the wicket and changed his team's style of play. He flicked the switch to power and thrashed the South Australian bowlers. His 50 came up in 43 minutes and, with Peter Toohey, he put on an 88-run partnership in an hour.

Gilmour hit 12 boundaries and reset the equation for the visitors who now needed 85 runs with six wickets in hand. Gilmour's play seemed fuelled by the contest. His spray of short balls when bowling was coupled now with hard hitting. He was seemingly determined to punish South Australia rather than just beat them.

Jenner needled him as he batted and the pair exchanged words. Jenner tossed one up and Gilmour pulled him so hard for four that fielders winced. If Jenner was playing a mind game then it worked next ball when Gilmour surged to mash another boundary only to mis-hit the shot. Woodcock at wide deep mid-off took a brilliant catch.

New South Wales seemingly had the match in its kit bag but there was exasperation in the rooms about the undisciplined dismissal. In the wake of Gilmour's innings, Toohey took over and played beautifully. Entering the final hour he and O'Keeffe put on 40.

Chappell had bowled Mallett almost all day, with his other bowlers rotated at the other end with little success. He rested

Prior (who had conceded eight off one over) and brought Cosier on. When O'Keeffe pushed defensively at Cosier's medium pace and was caught behind there were only 45 runs needed. When Rixon swept hard at Mallett and was caught at deep square-leg by Hookes, it was 38.

Toohey remained in command and whittled the target down to 22 when Chappell brought Prior back on. Prior bowled short and sharp. As the shadows of the Members Stand began creeping onto the oval, four days of irascible cricket was coming to a conclusion.

The fourth ball Prior delivered to Toohey was ferocious and the edge it generated needed everything Chappell had left in him this late in the match to snag it at first slip. The ball went over Yagmich's head but Chappell leapt into the air and caught it with one hand.

Pascoe, next in, scratched out his mark, surveyed the field, hunched down over his bat, heard the thud of a ball hitting pad and the screeching appeal, and saw the umpire's finger go up. David Hourn never got near the ball that shattered his stumps. Prior believed it was the fastest ball he had bowled to that stage.

His hat-trick gave South Australia victory by 21 runs and delivered an exclamation mark on a sweet upset victory the state hadn't enjoyed for years. There wasn't an excuse of a dodgy wicket or hometown decisions – Chappell's side had gone toe to toe with the big kids and knocked them off. The captain smelt something good brewing.

'It gave us impetus and the young guys all did something. Hookes got some runs, Cosier got a big score and Prior was young, fit and quick. We were steaming. Then we get about five guys reported in that game – it was absolutely ridiculous.'

The players were buying into the swagger of Chappell's leadership that invited a contest. It was what Viv Richards admired – being up-front and ready. It wasn't, however, always easy for those looking on. Many officials and past players had decried Chappell's style as national captain and labelled his team 'The Ugly Australians'. They now feared the same approach was infecting South Australia.

Frank 'Typhoon' Tyson, the former English fast bowler, was coaching Victoria and commentating for the ABC. He wrote that the South Australia–New South Wales game had given cricket a 'severe slap in the face'.

'It is, perhaps, one of the major tragedies of modern day cricket that first-class players no longer feel constrained by propriety on the field of play. It seems to be the age of cricketers doing their own thing, irrespective of what the world might think of them. They pay little heed to the influence that they, as senior models to be imitated by junior cricketers, wield in the formation of the coming cricketing generation.'

Chappell dismissed Tyson and others who disliked his style. He strongly believed in the demarcation of roles. Umpires controlled the game, he reasoned, and if they had a problem with a player then they should come to the captain and tell him. The captain would deal with it.

This scenario had already played out the previous summer when, during an Ashes Test, one of the Shield umpires, Robin Bailhache, told Chappell to stop Lillee swearing at England's wicketkeeper Alan Knott. Chappell knew that if *he* told Lillee to stop then he, Chappell, would be the one who had a problem.

'So I approach [Lillee] on the basis that Dennis is right and the umpire is wrong. I say, "Look, Dennis, the umpire is a pillock but he told me you were swearing at Knotty; for God's sake don't swear at Knotty. If you have something to get off your chest look at the ground and get cranky with yourself. I can't afford Bailhache to report you and you get suspended and miss a couple of games."'

The idea that such an incident should be reported and discussed later by administrators appalled him.

'Their criticism is fine coming from the air-conditioned committee room, [where they sit] with a gin and tonic in hand, but when you are out there trying to win then it's going to overheat from time to time. That is why there are umpires and captains.'

Swayed by the reporting of the 'Ugly Australians' and their frontier style of play, the Australian Cricket Board introduced paperwork in a bid to give umpires greater powers of regulation. In 1975–76 as umpires collected a new ball at the beginning of each match they were also given a report sheet should they need it. It offered them three areas to log any concerns: incidents on the field which were settled amicably; incidents in which the umpire intervened and which were not settled satisfactorily; and incidents which the umpire felt were detrimental to cricket.

Chappell hated them from the start, believing matters should be sorted out on the field. Whatever his thoughts on it, the South Australians almost filled the umpires' sheet after the first match. The umpires cited four players from South Australia (Chappell, Mallett, Jenner and Prior), and one from New South Wales (Gilmour), for their behaviour.

Among the grievances were Prior's threatening spray at McCosker, and Mallett and Chappell's chirping at O'Keeffe as he left the field after the first innings on 17 not out.

'Did you get your red ink okay, Skull?' they spat, knowing the spinner's love for being unbeaten.

When Chappell became aware that there would be an inquiry he told reporter Gordon Schwartz that 'they want to discuss the dropping-the-tweeds incident and my bowling'. They wanted more, though, including questioning his on-field language and that of his players. There was deep concern about the abrasive culture.

The bitterness between the captain and the selectors had been brewing for years. When Chappell arrived for a meeting before practice on Tuesday afternoon there were few niceties. He spent almost an hour in a session of raw character assessment with the panel of five, headed by South Australian Cricket Association president Phil 'Pancho' Ridings. They warned him that he was liable to be suspended if he was again reported for misconduct.

Chappell argued back. Although he wasn't reported for bowling full tosses, Ridings asked him why he had done it. Chappell explained his reasoning. Ridings asked what the difference it made between being 46 behind or 150 behind. Chappell exploded: 'If you don't know the difference then you don't know much about cricket.'

In his mind the captain worried about the fragility of his batting line-up. In previous seasons, collapses were regular and so there was concern that if the senior batsmen failed then the side could be all out for 150 runs or less.

'I told them I had had a gutful of what had been going on for the past two years. We were terrible and if we are terrible again this year then obviously I am not having much impact as a captain and so I will give it away and let someone else have a go.

'Phil says, "Why are you so angry about it? I finished last nine times." I said, "That is the fucking difference between you and me, Phil: I am not going to finish last nine years in a row."'

Schwartz watched Chappell storm out of the SACA offices and, unusually, refuse to make any comment to the gaggle of waiting journalists and cameramen. He went straight to the nets. His ire grew with every savage blow he dealt the bowlers.

His anger was down to both the lack of understanding and the lack of support from officials. South Australia had just scored its first significant victory in years and now he faced a panel tut-tutting about the atmospherics in which the game had been played. Chappell handled losses on the basis that they are inevitable if you play for a result – to win you have to risk losing. Two years of losing on the trot, however, wasn't something he was going to accept. And having pulled off a stunning opening victory after a strong showing against the West Indies he was now threatened with suspension. Chappell later said part of his love for the game died in the committee room that night.

When he finished in the nets he went into the change rooms and under a cold shower. Schwartz followed and with his notebook rapidly becoming a wet sponge he scribbled down that Chappell didn't want to comment because, 'I don't want to say anything while I'm in this mood that I may regret.'

When asked if he would continue as South Australian captain in view of his obvious hostility he replied: 'I haven't decided anything.'

*

The dramatic end to the New South Wales game was a talking point at Westbourne Park Primary School the next day with stories of Fang's hat-trick, Walters's injury and the South Australians on report growing more lurid with every retelling.

It wasn't the only news of the day. Our afternoon maths class was interrupted with an unscheduled visit from the headmaster. He was slightly flushed and more excitable than we had known him to be.

'I have something to tell you all,' he began. 'The Prime Minister has been sacked.'

With that he left and, for reasons unknown, the entire class burst out cheering.

CHAPTER THREE

BELIEF BEGINS TO STIR

South Australia v. Queensland, Adelaide, November 14–17, 1975

In late 2012 Ian Chappell was booked to speak at the Unley Town Hall and we agreed to meet beforehand in the council library next door. I was working on a story for the ABC after being contacted by Simon Smith, a specialist at the National Film and Sound Archive in Melbourne. He had recently digitised rare black and white film of an unofficial Australian cricket tour to North America in 1932. The film had been shot by a Canadian company on an unusual 28mm format and had been gathering dust for 80 years. The film was sent to Australia because its historic value was minimal in Canada compared with the excitement it generated in Australia, principally because it featured unseen footage of Don Bradman.

The tour had been privately arranged but sponsorship by the

Canadian Pacific Railway hinged on Bradman agreeing to come. Bradman was recently married and so turned the trip into a honeymoon of sorts. Jessie Bradman was the only woman among the 17-strong party.

Chappell was interested to see the film because it featured his grandfather, Vic Richardson. The action was filmed within the restrictions of cameras of the day but one shot showed Richardson in a social setting. He stared at the lens with the small grin of a man who knows that a lot is going on but who is not giving much away. There is a silent film star quality to him. The likeness to his grandson is striking.

'I was very fond of my grandfather,' Chappell said. 'When I read about him and hear stories about him I think, "Ahh, that's where it came from." I am more Richardson than Chappell.'

Speaking to the audience, Chappell returned to the theme, citing several stories about Richardson. In one, Richardson goes out to bat for South Australia against New South Wales in fading light at the Sydney Cricket Ground (SCG). The home side is a virtual Test XI and Richardson doesn't fancy a perilous few overs in murky conditions before stumps. He tells his batting partner, Jack 'Slinger' Nitschke, to follow him silently as he wanders toward fine leg. When the umpire Tommy Andrews asks him where he is going, Richardson replies in a loud voice, 'Call out again, Tommy, I can hear you but I can't see you'. The session was called off for bad light.

The crowd warmed as Chappell explained how his grandfather allowed him and his brothers room to develop, only phoning after a day's play to ask how they went before hanging up, or watching from afar when they played for Prince Alfred College. His occasional maxims were simple: don't swear at umpires; if you win the toss bat nine times out of ten and on the tenth time think about bowling and then bat; and if you ever captain Australia 'don't captain like a Victorian'.

Richardson played 19 Tests for Australia. He played in the Bodyline series where he advocated unsuccessfully for turning the tables and giving back to the Poms a bit of short stuff. He opposed the cable sent to the MCC by the Australian Board of Control decrying the tactics as 'unsporting' because he believed it looked like Australia was squealing about being beaten. In 1935 he captained Australia on a successful tour of South Africa, but when he returned he found Bradman had shifted to Adelaide and taken over as captain of both the state and the country.

'Vic was very careful at any family functions. If someone asked about Bradman he would say "great batsman" very abruptly and I always thought that was a sign not to ask any more questions. I always thought he didn't want to prejudice me; he wanted me to make up my own mind about Bradman. Little did he know his eldest daughter was white-anting him because my mother, Jeanne, was happy to state her opinion and generally it wasn't very complimentary.'

Cricket wasn't enough to keep Richardson contained, and he turned his hand to anything involving a contest – baseball, lacrosse and football. His winter home was a few hundred metres up the street from the library. At Unley Oval he was part of Sturt premiership sides and captained South Australia in the 1920s.

It was at this ground that his son-in-law, Martin Chappell, took his eldest son by the hand and walked up the stairs to the top of the grandstand where Lynn Fuller sat watching a district cricket match between Sturt and Glenelg. Fuller had played cricket in the forces during the war and was a sought-after coach. Martin Chappell introduced his son and asked if Fuller would consider giving him lessons.

'How old is he?'

'He is five.'

'Bring him around next Sunday.'

And so it started. Every week, from October through March, until he was 17, Ian Chappell would have a lesson in Fuller's backyard net. At the time plenty of suburban homes in Adelaide had tennis courts or cricket pitches in the backyard, usually surrounded by fruit trees, a galvanised iron rainwater tank on a brick stand and pergolas and sheds covered with sultana vines. Fuller taught him the shots and defence and then Martin told him how to make runs by throwing balls at odd angles and lengths at him. Make a decision, move your feet and play a shot for runs because you have to make runs to win games. As Greg later noted, Lynn gave them the strokes, Martin gave them the attitude.

Back home in the Chappell backyard there were no tennis balls, only cricket balls. Martin made a cricket pitch wide enough for three batsmen and protected the fruit trees with nets. He held fielding sessions but didn't lob catches, instead throwing them against walls and nets to create sharp angles and reflexes.

Martin was still playing grade cricket and Ian was always in the rooms. He didn't have to push him because the kid loved it. As a 13-year-old he began scoring for Glenelg and always wore his whites in case they were short. On one occasion they were and he filled in, batting at number nine and making a handful of runs in almost an hour at the crease. He was in awe of the opposition bowler 'Blue' Ballantyne.

Afterwards he was frozen out by his father on the drive home. Eventually he could take it no more. He asked what his father thought about the day. His father replied curtly he had seen him back away from Ballantyne's bowling and until he overcame this fear he wasn't playing C-grade again with the men.

Tough love at the Chappell household.

Greg was five years younger and as soon as he could compete he was named as England in Test matches against Australia (Ian). These were fully-enacted games where every batsman was named and batting style – left- or right-handed – replicated. Once a dismissal took place the batsman walked off into the laundry to record the score and returned as a new player.

The arguments were as combative as the sport. They blued over decisions and the state of the pitch. Victories were glorious and defeats unbearable. It was Australia and England played by the grandsons of a man who had opened the batting against Harold Larwood and Bill Voce. Which is why when they started playing together at club level, it was an odd experience. People expected them to have a sibling understanding but they had always opposed each rather than being team mates. The first time they batted together was in a semi-final for Glenelg against West Torrens and Ian worried about Greg. When all-rounder Neil Hawke trapped Greg lbw, Ian flew into a rage.

'I wanted to belt Hawkie because he was a Test cricketer and this was my little brother. For a while later I batted in anger but fortunately it was such a tight situation, and Glenelg were relying on me to win the semi-final for them, that I had to concentrate and get it out of my mind.'

The following week in the final, Ian was out for almost nothing but sat and watched Greg make a 50, and from that moment on he never worried about him again.

In addition to genetics, Richardson gave the boys a taste of the life the game provided. He was a raconteur and Ian noted his cricket stories were not about scores or results. Instead, his yarns were about the people he had met and the circumstances in which they found themselves.

His connections and those of Martin via Glenelg Cricket Club opened up some social opportunities to be around cricketers. The club had two former Test players – Gavin 'The Ox' Stevens and Graeme Hole – plus Murray Sargent who had played state cricket. When South Africa toured in 1952–53 they were entertained at Sargent's Seacliff home and the Chappells were invited.

The headmaster of Prince Alfred College, where Ian and Greg won scholarships, was Jack Dunning – a former New Zealand cricketer. When the Kiwis toured they gathered for an evening at his home on the school grounds.

When the Adelaide Test was played Martin would take Ian

and set his mind ticking. This wasn't a day of recreation but a chance to learn, especially from his father's favourites who tended to be aggressive and enthusiastic players.

'Watch Miller,' he told his son.

Martin admired Keith Miller. Ian watched him closely – his unpredictable deliveries and sheer athleticism stood out. He made things happen. He recalls him running for a sharp single and sliding his bat until it stuck in the turf. He would have skewered himself but instead hurdled the bat. Over the seasons there were others such as Johnny Martin, Frank Tyson and Les Favell.

'I think it was the whole package. I had grown up in an atmosphere where cricket was always around the house and we were always talking about cricketers.'

Force of opinion was a family strength. When Ian clashed with Martin it was a test of wills. If he came home late Martin would greet him on the front verandah demanding answers and questioning his commitment. Back and forth they would go. Greg preferred to let Martin win, with the prize being an extra hour's sleep. Once after a blue Martin hissed to Ian 'You are just like your bloody grandfather' after which he heard his mother's voice calling from another room – 'Don't you talk about my father like that'.

'That got me off the hook.'

Ian was Greg's hero and, he says, the best captain he played under. Ian set a path for him by working through district cricket, a stint in league cricket in England, Shield and then Test cricket – Ian's first Test cap coming against Pakistan in December 1964.

When Ian toured South Africa in 1966, Greg came into the South Australian side. The scoreboard attendants used the board they had made up for his brother when Greg came in to bat. When Ian returned to the side the attendants had a problem – how to distinguish between the brothers. So they created a new name board, CHAPPELL I, and a nickname was created.

Although their father was strong in his opinions he let the boys develop their own styles. Ian played back and across and loved hooking, pulling and cutting the ball, whereas Greg came forward and loved to drive. Ian was short and strong, Greg taller and graceful. Ian bowled leg spin while Greg was medium pace.

In 1972 at The Oval they made hundreds together under the gaze of their parents. Their younger brother, Trevor, played league cricket in England that winter and sat alongside his parents in admiration of his siblings.

During a rain delay, Ian was invited into the BBC broadcast booth to join Alan McGilvray and Brian Johnston. He used the opportunity to send a message of thanks to Lynn Fuller. Back home Fuller was listening on the radio and immediately wrote a letter of congratulations to the boys.

Greg had always believed he would live, play cricket and die in South Australia, but in the early 1970s he started getting growing pains. He vaguely considered the final step of following his brother by becoming Australian captain. It would be tough getting the gig sitting behind him and so he agreed to a lucrative offer to play in Queensland in 1973.

The first time the brothers were pitted against each other,

Greg faced both Ian and Trevor (who was in his first season of Shield cricket), and Martin who was acting as South Australian tour manager. Ian feared the worst considering his side 'couldn't beat time with a drum'.

He was right. The home side won by nine wickets despite a 126 by Ian in the second innings as he tried to save the game. Greg took four wickets and was bowling late when Ian was still at the crease supporting the tail. When Greg bounced number ten, Barry Hiern, Ian lost his rag. He hated seeing his tailenders bounced and always offered a challenging solution to the bowler: give them to me. It wasn't a trap Greg was falling for because he knew from the backyard how good his brother's hook shot was. He told him to worry about batting and he would worry about bowling.

Ashley Woodcock was at school with Greg and knew the family well. He saw them both being intensely competitive, determined and smart.

'With Greg you couldn't always detect it but Ian you could because he wore his heart on his sleeve.'

When the South Australians limped home Ian received a phone call from his mother. After commiserating, she asked after Greg and how it had gone captaining against each other. Ian reported they had been arguing within five minutes of the game starting.

'What took so long?' she replied.

*

For Trevor Chappell the path to first-class cricket was well-worn but difficult to traverse. Like the others he went through the cricket academy at Fuller's backyard and Prince Alfred College where he rewrote the record books. The school coach, Chester Bennett, whose gentle guidance had steered all three boys, thought at that stage that Trevor showed the most promise of them all.

When he was 12, Trevor saw Ian's new baggy green cap and jumper that had arrived in advance of his first Test match. He had seen so many photos of men wearing that kit and now he was only outstretched fingers away from one in his own home. The temptation to try them on was palpable but he resisted in the superstitious belief that somehow it might bugger up his chance of ever having his own.

A successful stint in England was followed by selection for South Australia where he started well, scoring several half-centuries in his first year. Trevor thought in hindsight that the pressure to perform in Adelaide was greater than he sensed at the time.

By 1975 he was struggling. Against the West Indies he made 5 and 17 not out. Batting at number five against New South Wales he made a pair. Despite the thrilling victory he couldn't enjoy the celebrations because a cloud of failure was hanging over him. He had scored over 1,000 runs and taken 100 wickets in England but couldn't get going at home. He asked Dennis Yagmich if he could spend the night at his house where he slept on the wicketkeeper's couch. Like Greg he couldn't imagine playing anywhere but Adelaide but later he and Yagmich discussed grade cricket in Perth, a conversation that eventually saw him move to Western Australia.

Trevor idolised his two brothers but was caught between their styles. One night after training he drove home with Ian down Anzac Highway and talked about how confused he felt. He liked to play the short balls like Ian but was trying to be a free-striker like Greg. Ian said he had to work out what sort of player he was and play like that – it was a mental block.

'It was the first time I'd really thought about how I should play, other than trying to be like Ian and Greg.'

He came to the conclusion he was a 'nicker and a nudger' who could survive in the middle. After the New South Wales game he spoke to Mike Coward who was working for the *Advertiser,* telling him there were times when he wished – only in a cricketing sense – that he wasn't a Chappell. He had done well in England because he was 'on his own' and he confirmed that there were times he considered quitting the sport.

He didn't and in years to come played Test cricket for Australia. He found it frustrating that people didn't acknowledge how much work it took to reach that height but he preferred to reflect on the rarity of four Test cricketers, and three Australian captains, all coming from one family.

But for now it all seemed too much. Shortly after the interview with Coward ended the selectors confirmed he had been dropped from the side. The 23-year-old would never play for South Australia again.

Trevor Chappell's place in the South Australian side was taken by Rick Darling, a teenager whose cricket lineage went back further than Vic Richardson. Joe Darling was a left-handed opener who made his Test debut before Federation. He was cleaned bowled first ball at the SCG by Tom Richardson of England. Despite his poor start in Test cricket Darling had a brilliant career and toured England four times, three times as captain of Australia.

He was an imposing Edwardian figure wearing the pre-baggy skull cap of Australia and sporting a moustache that was clipped like a box hedge. That was the image that sat framed above the fireplace in the homestead in which his great-nephew, Rick, grew up. Joe Darling died in 1945, the year the government started handing out blocks of land and access to the River Murray for irrigation to men returning from the war.

One such citrus block – at Ramco, in South Australia's Riverland – provided Rick the venue for an idyllic childhood, one in which he played among the trees and swam in the river. Cricket was his passion and the boy would race home from school in time to sit in front of the black and white television to catch the final session of Shield or Test matches. He loved seeing Doug Walters on the telly and the picture of his famous ancestor framed on the wall.

'I used to sit in front of the fire looking at that photo for what seemed like hours. I still have that photo.'

When Joe Darling was playing, South Australia was a rural place and Adelaide a small city. The majority of people lived and worked in the country, a life that revolved around farming. When the Depression hit, Premier Tom Playford, himself an orchardist, decided on a dramatic new direction. He coaxed, teased and bribed industry into setting up in South Australia. He took control of the state's electricity and built public housing for workers. Through rent and wage controls he offered cheap labour to large companies. Soon Adelaide, Port Augusta and Whyalla became industrial hubs and the city-country divide started swinging around. By the early 1960s more people lived in Adelaide than the country.

Cricketers, no matter how good they were in country competitions, would never get a look in for first-class cricket until they were tested in the city. That is why Darling left Ramco as a teenager to have a go with Salisbury, which was the district club furthest from the CBD and closest to the river.

He got a job in a sports store and boarded with the family of another young player making his way at the club. Wayne Prior and his parents were wonderful people but Darling yearned for his country home. The homesickness became so acute he abandoned the city after a few months – but not his path to top cricket. Instead, every week he travelled the four-hour round trip from Ramco to Salisbury. During the week he practiced at home with his cousins Wayne and Don on a malthoid synthetic pitch.

In only his second full season of A-grade, Darling became the first player living in the country to be picked in the state side since Brian Hurn in 1957. In doing so, Darling added to one of Australian cricket's most-loved narratives – written so boldly by Bradman – of the country kid who comes down from his own dunghill to town where he hits with a freedom and strength borne of another landscape. A sporting gift from the earth.

Darling was brave, stylish and fast. He could hook and cut and could run singles others wouldn't attempt. His unbeaten 48 in a South Australian Colts XI against the West Indies in their first match of the 1975–76 tour suggested to the selectors that the 18-year-old might be ready.

He might not have seemed ready to those listening to the sound of him vomiting in the rooms before going out to bat. Although initially alarmed by it, soon the team accepted that this was part of Darling's ritual as much as putting on his pads. Yagmich found him having a chunder at the warm up nets once. Darling thinks that the number of times it happened over the years has been exaggerated but is happy to own up to it.

'I found it sharpened me up a bit actually.'

Darling had taken the phone call from the South Australian selectors in the Waikerie office of the Electricity and Water Supply Department, where he was a trainee surveyor. He was to play in the second Shield match of the season, against Queensland. He drove to town on Thursday after work and asked the Priors if he could stop with them for the four days.

The next morning, when Darling came into the home rooms at the Adelaide Oval, he was apprehensive knowing he had replaced the captain's brother in the line-up.

'It could have gone badly but Ian couldn't have been better to me. He made me feel very welcome. He was basically captain and coach of South Australia. He had a big job. We only travelled with a team manager, so Ian captained, coached, talked to the press, along with many other responsible tasks. He had been doing it for a long time.'

Chappell put the teenager at cover or in the outfield where he immediately became popular with the bowlers because he cut off boundaries. His pace added to the growing enthusiasm of the team.

Greg Chappell had won the toss and followed his grandfather's edict. The innings went sour quickly and Queensland was dismissed for 188. Terry Jenner took 5/73 and Ashley Mallett 3/32 in steaming conditions. The visitors collected only one batting point while South Australia collected five bowling points.

Ashley Woodcock strained a thigh muscle in the field and so was put down the order, bringing Chappell up to open with Drewer. There was only time for a few overs before stumps and as the South Australians padded up there was only one thing on their mind – Jeff Thomson.

*

For two summers Thomson–Lillee were the Jagger–Richards of world cricket and, like Mick and Keith, their popular, high-octane act was delivered with a calculated menace. They were fast and aggressive and set fans on edge. Batsmen had a flashing moment to make a decision. A miscalculation led to bruising, bleeding and breaking.

They came together to destroy England in 1974–75, and in 1975–76 it was the West Indies' turn. Viv Richards referred to them respectfully in the collective: 'They were the man.'

The two moments when Ian Chappell realised what forces were at play both took place in Perth, home to the nation's fastest deck. In December 1971 Lillee took 8/29 against a rest-of-the-world team that included Garry Sobers, Tony Greig and Sunil Gavaskar. So devastating was his display that the innings was over within a session and the tourists put back in. Lillee struck again and, in doing so, gave Indian opener Farokh Engineer the unlikely-to-be-repeated dishonour of being dismissed twice before lunch.

Chappell thought that when Lillee came into bowl that day he looked like a man in a hurry, one trying to elbow his way through a crowd. That tearaway action changed after his back could take no more in the Caribbean in 1973. Lillee honed his technique to protect himself from further injury. He had a Spartan approach to training and willed himself with every delivery. The whirlwind arms and long run-up of his first incarnation were slowly chiselled down. The length of his run-up, the angle of his leading elbow, the height of his leap, and the position of his chin and eye line were all examined. He re-emerged with a precise action where the only thing not in control was his Medusa hair and the gold medallion swinging from a chain around his neck.

Greg Chappell believed Lillee wasn't a natural athlete but had the capacity to make himself great. Lillee studied the mechanics, geometry and physics of bowling. Like a Zen master of a volcanic craft, he would put his name to a book called *The Art of Fast Bowling*. He started with an out-swinger and added an off-cutter before learning the leg-cutter from English pace bowler John Snow.

If Lillee could describe every link in the chain of his delivery, Thomson's summary of his approach was less precise: 'I just shuffle in and go wang.' He was a free spirit in a game of ritual and stricture and carried himself with the confidence that comes from natural talent. He was an athlete in the classical sense – fast, lithe and coordinated. At school his legend grew from the time he first picked up a javelin and went 'wang'. He was soon state champion. His return throws from the boundary bruised the hands of the wicketkeeper as much as his deliveries.

Chappell's second fast-bowling epiphany was when Thommo unleashed a delivery against England at the WACA in 1974. It was short and fast. To describe it, Chappell gestures with his arm and makes the motion of a jet aircraft taking off: 'Whoosh!'

The ball seared the batsman as it went past. The slip cordon twisted their necks to see it disappearing and heard the bang as it hit the sightscreen on the half volley. It is likely it travelled 75 metres. As the fielders turned their gaze back to the wicket, Chappell looked at the batsman and saw the blood drain from his face.

At the Gabba, at the beginning of that Ashes series, Greig had taken on the fast bowlers and fashioned a brilliant century.

In doing so, he taunted the Australians, signalling his own fours and stirring them at every opportunity. It worked. The bowling kept getting shorter and more undisciplined.

Set 332 to win, Greig again came to the crease and Thommo bounced him before sending down a screaming yorker. The ball hit Greig's shoe, which had a rubber soul, and went onto the stumps. As the players gathered in a huddle to congratulate their bowler Chappell seized the moment to suggest that maybe in future it was better to try to knock Greig's stumps over than knock his block off.

Someone said, 'Nah, hit him in the sandshoe, Thommo'.

Thomson loved it and asked them: 'You want to see more of the sandshoe crusher?' which was followed by a unanimous cry of 'Yes!'

Unlike most young men who are good at all sports, Thomson chose cricket because he found it the easiest. His first love was surfing and he would turn up for cricket training at Bankstown in Sydney's west with his high school mate Len Pascoe, wearing board shorts and brushing sand off his feet to put his boots on. He gave up playing professional rugby because it required more effort than cricket where 'you just turned up and played without even trying'.

He hated batsmen and held the belief that if they knew how to bowl they would be bowlers, not batsmen. He also hated talking about bowling, as if somehow caring too much would take away the magic.

'I just loved to see the ball go zing through somebody and

no matter how good they thought they were they weren't quick enough to get near it. That is what really turned me on and that is what scared the hell out of them because they were doing their best and they were a bit late.

'I just made sure the seam was up – I didn't worry about the swing and all this slower ball crap – I just enjoyed fast bowling.'

With his attitude came a natural disdain for authority which fitted perfectly into the ethos of the Australian team. He called blokes who wore suits and club ties 'crawlers'. His respect for Chappell was because he was a number-three batsman who took on the quicks.

His first taste of Test cricket was a disaster, bowling 19 expensive and wicket-less overs against Pakistan at the Melbourne Cricket Ground (MCG) in December 1972. His rebellion had worked against him because he had an undiagnosed broken bone in his foot which he hid from the selectors. When the injury healed he found he wasn't included in the New South Wales side.

When he eventually was picked for the final match of the 1973–74 season it was at the SCG against Queensland. By now, Thommo was seriously cheesed off with the state selectors for overlooking him and, in his opinion, playing inferior bowlers instead.

'You look around, you sum everyone up and think if I am not better than them then I will give it away. I am not one who sits back and cops it, it just fires me up more and I proved a point.'

He took 7/85 in the first innings and 2/40 in the second as the Blues won by 167 runs. Thomson had always got on well with

Greg Chappell and in the rooms afterwards Chappell suggested that if the bowler was peeved with his home state there was an offer to head north. Thomson's immediate thought was not cricket but fishing because as a kid his family had spent holidays in Queensland. He also thought being on the same team as Chappell meant he wouldn't have to bowl to him – a rare sign of respect for a batsman.

'Greg understood me. He knew I was an outdoors bloke and pretty casual. I probably do a lot of things everyone else would want to do and I get away with them a bit more. We would be getting ready for a season and he knew I was up the Barrier Reef fishing. He would say, "For goodness sake, get down here. They are giving me a hard time." I lived in a motel but never spent much time there. I was at the Queensland Cricketers' Club playing snooker or cards.'

He saved some extra venom for his old state, sending a message to the selectors by taking it out on former team mates, including Doug Walters.

'You didn't know where the ball was which was an advantage for Thommo,' says Walters.

'We were taught as kids to watch the ball in the bowler's hand as he was running in, and with a lot of bowlers you can actually see it from the time they went back to the top of their mark until it comes out of their hands.

'With Thommo it was coming around from the back and, particularly in his early days, he wasn't very accurate, so you had no idea. I have a vision span down the wicket about 18 inches wide, so if the ball comes into that vision you can do something with it. Sometimes Thommo would bowl and it wouldn't be in that vision span. It was wide outside off-stump or all the way down the leg side. Sometimes I wasn't too sure he had even let it go because of that action and you have to face a lot of that sort of bowling to get used to it.'

Many of the West Indians had watched television footage in England of the destruction Thommo wreaked in the Ashes series of 1974–75. Clive Lloyd says they were very, very aware of what he could do, describing his bowling as 'dangerous'. How much it played on the tourists' minds cannot be known but several times during their stay in South Australia early in the tour, Lloyd made a point of denying his batsmen were in awe or frightened of Australian bowlers. Richards says any batsman who faced Thomson had to deal with the fear inside of them.

After Queensland had been dismissed for 188 in 60.5 overs, the wang-master let them fly late on the first day against South Australia, capturing Drewer for one and Chappell for nine in two overs. Ashley Mallett went in as a night watchman and he and Gary Cosier survived until quarter to six when, mercifully, they were given the light. South Australia 2/26.

Mallett hung around the next morning reaching 34 before – shuffle, wang, click, thump – he nicked Thomson and was caught behind by John Maclean. Woodcock was on two when he tried to drive Thommo and watched his mistimed shot spoon to David Ogilvie at cover.

Cosier was at the crease when Darling arrived for his first-class debut. Because the batsmen hadn't crossed, Darling had to face and so he scratched out his mark and looked around the field. He heard the umpire say 'right arm over, six to come'.

'I looked up and here comes Jeff Thomson. With Thommo it was either going to be a bouncer or a yorker. He tried a yorker and I got a thick inside edge and it went down to backward square.'

He had survived the sandshoe crusher and Cosier absorbed the next five balls. The next over couldn't have been more of a contrast, with the ball given to leg-spinner Malcolm Francke. Darling danced down the wicket and drove him wide of mid-wicket for three. Next over, a Thomson fireball went to point for a single.

Cosier then drove Thomson to mid-on where Denis Schuller misfielded. Schuller was also a product of Salisbury Cricket Club but had moved to Queensland for more opportunities. Seeing Schuller fumble, Darling took off and the batsmen crossed for one before hesitating. The teenager's speed would get him back but he looked to the senior partner for a sign. They went for the run but the moment of indecision bought enough time for Schuller to gather the ball and his return shattered the stumps at the non-striker's end as Darling dived in vain. He was face down, spread-eagled on the Adelaide Oval pitch.

The startling piece of fielding, along with Thommo's ferocity, left South Australia at 5/68, still 120 runs behind Queensland. Such batting collapses were hallmarks of recent seasons. Hours of hard work were eroded in minutes as wickets fell, and with them came questions about technique, application or even the ability to compete at this level against bigger states. It was one reason why the selectors, with the approval of Chappell, were playing the kids.

As a teenager departed, a 20-year-old came to the crease but David Hookes at least didn't have to face Thomson straight away. Cosier was settled and, as the day drew on, Thomson's influence faded. If in the past more wickets would have been lost then here was some sign that things were changing.

Cosier and Hookes played aggressively, batting at a run per minute. As their partnership grew Queensland's momentum stalled and, as Hookes twice belted Francke for six over the mid-wicket boundary, the game swung South Australia's way.

Watching from the other end Cosier was dazzled by Hookes's self-belief.

'Francke kept bowling wrong 'uns and Hookes would play and miss, bowl a wrong 'un again and he would play and miss. Then he bowled a leg spin and he hit him over the Victor Richardson Gates. Then wrong 'un ... miss, wrong 'un ... miss, leggie bang over Vic Richardson – he hit two sixes and would have missed four balls. He didn't care. He never worried about what had gone before. He was extremely confident.'

When Hookes was caught behind off Francke for 53 the pair had put on 85 for the sixth wicket. It was the innings that convinced Chappell that Hookes would make it at this level. Cosier kept on with the tail before being run out for 59. The innings ended at 248 – a lead of 60.

The excitement Cosier generated while batting with Hookes flowed into the field as South Australia pressured Queensland late on Saturday afternoon. Sam Trimble was caught by Cosier off Prior for four. Jenner bowled David Ogilvie for 13 and then Ian Davis was snagged at first slip by Chappell off Geoff Attenborough for 25.

Queensland was leading the Sheffield Shield competition and was unbeaten so far in three games. It had never won the title and its form made it the favourites to break the drought. But this stop in Adelaide was not going to plan. As the South Australians knocked the tops off the longnecks in the rooms that evening they had Queensland 3/61 – just one run ahead. After so much gloom for so long they were eyeing a possible second outright win.

The twin appeal of Thomson and Greg Chappell aroused the interest of cricket followers. A solid working-day crowd on Friday of almost three thousand was followed by nine thousand over the weekend. The Adelaide crowds were divided into members and non-members and with them came a cultural difference. Theatre critic Peter Goers referred to the Members as 'the Adelaide Club with a front lawn'. They tended to be conservative in outlook and their entitlement sometimes included offering advice to players as they came and went from the change rooms through the stand. Chappell would often answer them back. The players' room was not glassed in, so members could turn in their seats and pass comments to him as he sat looking out. Cosier remembers Chappell telling them to shut up while pointing out the game was being played out there. When Barry Curtin was out first ball against Victoria he trudged up the stairs only to have a member crow at him: 'You are going the wrong way – the pitch is out there.' Curtin had to use every fibre of self-restraint to avoid using his bat in all the wrong ways and instead he glared long and hard at the man before continuing his walk.

The outer housed supporters more likely to be blue-collar city workers or university students – types who would choose on a whim to visit the oval if they sensed excitement. Chappell preferred this crowd and believed they were often more educated about the game than the members. It was a view shared by Thomson who said, 'You can't fool the public. They know good cricket.'

But there was a suspicion the crowds were unimpressed with the SACA's decision in 1975 to ban them bringing alcohol into the ground. In the past spectators would load up an esky with cans and work their way through them while lying on the grass underneath the scoreboard. Now, in addition to the $1.50 entry fee, they had to go to the bar to buy drinks.

The policy change was an attempt to wind down some of the larrikin behaviour that had been growing at matches – particularly Test matches. Crowd noise and fights were one thing but in recent seasons fans had thrown cans onto the field, grabbed fielders across the fence and taken off their togs to streak across the pitch. At the Ashes Test in Adelaide in January 1975 the gates had to be closed with only 30,000 fans inside (half the capacity) because there were so many eskies taking up space on the hills. Police had pushed for the grog ban but the SACA accountants were growing nervous when only 9,000 people watched over four days against New South Wales.

Shield matches were break-even affairs for the SACA. Its finances came from membership fees, sponsors, broadcast rights and international matches. Of the four state matches it would lose money on those against New South Wales and Victoria but make some against Western Australia and Queensland. The lure of Greg Chappell and Thomson made this contest the most lucrative of the domestic summer, raising $2,338 to tip the balance of Shield games into the black by $971 at season's end. This modest profit reduced the cost of running the state side to $17,980.

On Sunday morning, as the bells of St Peter's Cathedral pealed out over North Adelaide, several thousand spectators watched John Maclean trapped lbw by Prior for a duck. It effectively made Queensland 4/9. Out strode Greg Chappell in front of his former home crowd to try to salvage something for his adopted state. His innings was imperious. It wasn't a moment for heavy hitting and so he found the boundary only five times. Instead he played the ball to all parts using his elegant strokes. The South Australians appealed for every chance and niggled with gamesmanship. Chappell took no notice having long ago endured his brother's sledging in the backyard, and learnt to ignore it.

Ian Chappell's best chance was to rob his brother of partners. He turned to Mallett and, virtually, gave him one end for the day. The offie only had two overs of rest. He bowled mostly in tandem with Jenner who was occasionally spelled by the quicks.

Martin Kent was the breakthrough wicket when Mallett got him lbw for 33 in a partnership of 69. Next was Phil Carlson for 21 with the score at 193 – a lead of 133. Greg Chappell was one run from a century when Mallett baffled him momentarily and an edge went to Ian at first slip. Greg's huge wicket exposed the Queensland tail and when Francke became Mallett's fourth victim, Queensland was all out for 229. Between them, Mallett (4/58) and Jenner (3/67) had bowled 56 of the 75 overs.

South Australia had time on Sunday evening to put a dent in the 170 it needed to win but, as in the first innings, facing Thommo after a day in the field was unenviable at best. It became perilous when Drewer didn't get through Thomson's first over. Woodcock fared better and was 26 when he was brilliantly caught by Schuller at point. Chappell and Cosier grafted until stumps, leaving South Australia with 98 to win on the final day.

More than one thousand people turned up on a Monday to see if the new South Australia would take a remarkable win or the old South Australia would wilt in the face of Thomson. They were surprised that Greg Chappell rested his strike weapon, but Thomson's back wasn't right and his captain would need him for more important games than this one. Without him Queensland caused only minor damage. Cosier was caught behind for 49 and Darling was not out one. Four overs before lunch, Ian Chappell walked off the field unbeaten on 89. South Australia had won.

He said in the rooms afterwards that the match had given him more pleasure than any state game for years. He sensed greater fitness and stamina in his team but, most significantly, he saw a mental strength appearing. With 37 points from two games Chappell said publicly for the first time what he had said to the team before the season – that they could win the Sheffield Shield. They were still well behind Queensland who topped the table, but South Australia had only played two games while Queensland had now played four.

Just like in the backyard, he had it over his little brother. Next up was the state he hated more than any other.

CHAPTER FOUR

NEW BLOOD AND AN OLD ENEMY

Victoria v. South Australia, Melbourne, December 5–8, 1975

In some sense the 1960s arrived in South Australia in the 1970s. The political and social restlessness of Woodstock and the counter-culture of other western countries was more a curiosity than a reality in a state noted for its conservatism. State premier Tom Playford, the orchardist from the Adelaide Hills who embraced manufacturing, created a record in the British Commonwealth for political longevity by serving 26 years and 126 days in office.

He was helped by a corrupt electoral system that gave disproportionate representation to country voters ahead of those in the city. They tended to vote conservatively. In 1965 the weight of numbers in the city finally ended his innings, with former stonemason Frank Walsh elected to lead a Labor Government. The trouble for Labor was that Frank was 67 years old and, like the rest of the cabinet, had waited a lifetime to get the keys to the cabinet room. The exception was a brilliant young lawyer, Don Dunstan, who started as Walsh's attorney general and soon took over as premier. When he was asked what he intended doing, he replied: 'Return South Australia to its Chartists' roots.'

He was referring to the political movement of the early 19th century in England that agitated for a charter to protect the rights of working-class men and women. It was the same time and atmosphere that generated the South Australian Company – a mob determined to settle a new colony along radical political lines known as systematic colonisation. It involved free settlers and enlightened democracy, and pioneered many ideals, such as universal suffrage (including women voting and standing for parliament), land title, juvenile justice and taxation.

Things didn't always go to plan, however, and economically the colony got the wobbles early and often. But fortunes turned around when a mother lode of copper was discovered at Burra, north of Adelaide, in the 1840s. The men who did the digging were mostly from Cornwall – typically Methodist, hard-working and proud. Along the way they battled those paying poor wages. Knowing what the ore was worth, many organised for a deal that included a slice of the profits. Among them were the ancestors of the Chappells.

Although the radical visions of the pioneers had been diluted and sidelined during decades of conservative rule, Dunstan believed they remained just below the surface and he unleashed them during his decade in power.

South Australia was socially and politically off to the races. He ripped through the statute books changing consumer affair laws: licensing laws were relaxed, the voting age was lowered, laws protecting women and minorities were enshrined, education was revamped and the arts was treated as an industry not a hobby.

The atmosphere made for radical thought and action. South Australia became the first place in the country to decriminalise homosexuality, appoint a woman to the Supreme Court, and grant Indigenous land rights. It was the centre of the renaissance of Australian cinema. Arts colleges sprung up. In 1971 an Indigenous group of activists designed a flag of red and black with a yellow circle in the centre that became the symbol of pride across the country. A Yorta Yorta man, Douglas Nicholls, was appointed governor.

Dunstan led from the front with panache. He took on protest crowds in the street with a loud hailer and baited and outwitted his opponents in parliament. He liked safari suits and cravats and wore a T-shirt, shorts and long socks to parliament. He recited poetry, acted in theatre productions, gardened and put out a cookbook. His second wife was Malaysian journalist Adele Koh and he championed multiculturalism. His style and verve affected others including Gough Whitlam with whom he had worked to rid Labor of its support for the White Australia Policy. Neville Wran in New South Wales and John Cain in Victoria looked on with curiosity and envy.

In 1975 the wheels came off Whitlam's experiment in Canberra. After a bitter campaign Malcolm Fraser led the Liberal

Party back to office. Dunstan campaigned as best he could for the ALP but the tide was turning. The post-war promise of full employment was becoming a myth as jobs became scarce while wages growth pushed inflation into double digits.

The mood of the day was turbulent – traditional patterns were being questioned and changed – driven by restlessness, particularly of young people who weren't as accepting as their war-time parents had been. Ian Chappell's Australians fitted right into this environment; they were brash, talented and questioning of authority. Even the fashion of playing with their shirts opened to the middle of their chests seemed a challenge to a previous, buttoned-up age.

Richie Benaud recognised a difference in the relationships between administrators and players in the 1970s that outpaced other eras. When Chappell was given an appointment to meet the Australian Cricket Board (the new name for the Australian Board of Control) to discuss playing conditions and payments he sought Benaud's advice. Benaud was envious because in his time as captain he was never afforded such an opportunity. He advised Chappell to write an agenda to force the board to take minutes.

The meeting turned sour once an increase in players' remuneration was broached. It was Sir Donald Bradman – silent on all other matters – who answered any agenda items about increased payments. His dead bat blocked any possibility of an increase.

'The ACB were the ones very much in charge of the game but some people's habits started to change and people started to question things,' said Benaud in a reflective interview with Mike Coward in 2001.

'If [in the 1950s] someone would say, "That's the way things should be" ... you would say, "Oh yeah, okay." But in the 70s it was much more confrontational. People would say "why?" and then they would go away and think about it, then come back and have another discussion and say, "Hang on a second, that's not right [or] what we were told the other day."

'I think it was a big difference there in the 70s and perhaps the late 60s as well. Quite different from when I started with players who had come back from the war. I think you could definitely underline that people in the 70s were in that position where we weren't.'

In 1972 Chappell confronted Bradman about money, this time on behalf of his South Australian team mates. Chappell believed the state only had about a dozen first-class players and so couldn't afford to lose any. However, all-rounder Ken 'KG' Cunningham and opener John Causby decided they couldn't continue because they were getting pressure from their work places for being away so often. If the money for Test cricketers was meagre then it was breadline for state players.

At the time each player received $8 per day plus $2.50 for an evening meal, less tax. On one trip to Sydney, the South Australians were invited to a barbecue by the Cricketers' Club of New South Wales. The SACA docked them their meal allowance.

Chappell expected his players to give him every effort on the field and so believed the other side of that coin was that he would look after them off it. They were his boys, he used to say.

Chappell sought a resolution to the impending loss of Cunningham and Causby. After research with AMP, he proposed a superannuation-type scheme that wouldn't cost the SACA much money but would build a financial incentive for the players when they retired. He met Bradman in his city office armed with information and hope. It went badly.

'I get harangued by him – away he went. I walked out thinking, "Ian, did you just go into that meeting and put your wallet on the table and ask Sir Donald to fill it up?" I could take the easy way out because [tobacco company] WD & HO Wills paid me, so I was one of few who were reasonably well-off for those times, but to me the job of the captain is to fight for his players. I got the feeling Bradman treated the board money almost as if it was his money.'

For many players the thrill of playing first-class cricket overshadowed any financial desires. The common theme was that if you were given one of those caps you would play for free. Equally, others whose place in the side was at times marginal, feared that getting bolshie about money could jeopardise things further.

Chappell knew they were being exploited in the sense that there was a tremendous discrepancy between what their services were worth and what they were being paid. That to play state cricket was something others desperately wanted to do shouldn't come into the equation.

Standing at first slip one day at the MCG, Chappell turned to Barry Curtin and said, 'Look at the crowd, Bazz.'

'Yeah, it's a good crowd,' Curtin replied.

'Where do you think the money is going?'

At other times he pointed out that the barman at the Adelaide Oval was getting $25 per day while the players were getting half that, plus a longneck and a carton of Benson and Hedges.

'We are the ones providing the entertainment. I have never seen a crowd come here to watch the administrators play,' Chappell would say.

The South Australian administrators stood accused of falling behind. They couldn't match the offer made to Greg Chappell that saw him go north. During the lunch break on the Saturday of the 1975 match in Melbourne, the South Australian players became aware that recently retired Victorian Peter Bedford was being presented with a cheque for $900 – his provident fund payout.

The only concession the SACA made to the Age of Aquarius was changing its cap. South Australia's traditional navy blue baggy caps were replaced by tight-fitting red baseball-style numbers with a motif featuring the state's piping shrike emblem.

It was the cap that David Hookes received and it signalled the arrival of a talent that was equal parts extraordinary and enigmatic.

The swirling, radicalised 1970s were often bewildering times for him as a young man growing up in Adelaide's western suburbs, but it was the structure of sport that gave him solace and direction. Hookes lived close to Thebarton Oval and its twin forces of football and cricket. In Adelaide District Cricket some clubs – Glenelg, Port Adelaide, Sturt, Prospect (North Adelaide), Woodville and West Torrens – were associated with football.

In the winter game the players of the West Torrens Eagles wore a magnificent, royal-blue guernsey featuring the outline of a golden eagle in full flight across the chest. Although the ground was fashioned from an old clay quarry and lived up to its nickname the 'Pughole', it consistently produced players known for their deft touch and adventurous play. In the summer game West Torrens had been home to Test players including Ron Hamence, Merv Waite and Neil Hawke.

Hookes loved the ground and its combatants, so much so that his older brother, Terry, called him 'the Thebby Oval kid'. He pulled on the eagle guernsey and played in an Under-17s grand final on the Adelaide Oval in 1973, but cricket was the game in which he excelled.

It began when his mother Pat grabbed his arm and marched him to the front of a gaggle of boys at a net session being run by A-grade batsman Denis Brien.

'This is my son David and he wants to play cricket,' she said.

The coach looked at the kid's blond hair and then his bare feet. This could be a problem.

The arches of his feet tilted from inside to the outside while one leg was shorter than the other. Consequently his legs were severely bowed. The orthopaedic specialist gave the family two options – leg irons or going barefoot. They chose the latter and so the boy's first day of school was the first time he wore shoes.

He did have his own bat (which was smaller than the other

kids'). He then produced a pair of spikes from his little bag and put them on, assuming he was now ready.

Brien kept spare gear and so kitted him out with pads, gloves and a box. He liked him and encouraged him to follow his instincts and use his gift. As Hookes advanced, people wanted Brien to correct his style, especially his footwork. His reply was 'God knows more than me and he put it in so I am not taking it out.'

'I think if we had corrected him more he would have been a very, very good A-grader but allowing him to have flair he became a charismatic player.'

Away from cricket, things were not always easy at Hookes's home as his parents' divorce played out bitterly. At one stage almost a decade passed where he had no contact with his dad and so Brien became a surrogate father. The Brien family, and by extension his club, put enormous hairy arms around the boy. Once, when being interviewed about the development of cricketers, Hookes drifted back to his own experiences as a teenager growing up in the turbulent early 1970s.

'I wouldn't like to have been outside a team environment in that generation. I remember as a 14-year-old playing C-grade at West Torrens and going to training on Thursday nights. [I'd] do some homework for an hour and then go to training then come back and do more homework.

'The older players there who played first-class cricket would be playing cards waiting for the team to be announced and they would let me have half a glass of beer. I would walk home. My parents knew that and allowed that – there was no clandestine swigging of beer out of a bottle. It was "Young fellow, go and get the beers and bring them over here and, yes, you can have half a glass."

'So you were surrounded by strong men who were thoughtful people and family people and basically, as a young, single child, that was my family. It was only two streets from home and I lived there in summer and I lived there in winter for football.

'So you could cope with all that [turmoil] because you had an extended family. I don't think I would have liked to have been an individual person with no team involvement anywhere, growing up at that time.'

Hookes's technique was based on his phenomenal eye. Rodney Hogg was fielding for Woodville in a game against West Torrens when he watched Hookes launch a ball high over the top of the grandstand. He was staggered at how cleanly and effortlessly – like Hookes had merely flicked it – the ball had been struck.

Hookes reminded Chappell of the South African left-hander Graeme Pollock who generated power through exquisite timing. When he came into the South Australian team Chappell found him confident but respectful. Hookes found the state rooms weren't the same as those at West Torrens.

Chappell was of the opinion that first-class cricket was not an education camp. If you were selected for South Australia then you should know how to play cricket. If you didn't, then you should go back to grade cricket and learn.

Hookes said: 'This old adage that the senior players looked after the younger players and took them through practising and change rooms is nonsense, really, because unless you went to the senior player then nothing was forthcoming – or rarely was something forthcoming.

'Ian never came to me with guidance on footwork or how to play the spinners or how to play fast bowling but I felt comfortable enough with him that I went to him quite a lot. As time went on Ian trusted my judgement as a player and knew that he could throw me into the deep end to sink or swim and if I felt I needed a life jacket I could come and ask for one.'

While most of the South Australians followed Chappell rapturously, no-one bought into his style more than Hookes. He watched his captain going to press conferences with a cigar and a beer, he listened to his salty tirades and saw him drop his dacks at the wicket. If a coat-tugger asked for an autograph in the bar Chappell would tell them to piss off and so would Hookes.

'We were encouraged to speak up and encouraged to say things and encouraged to have a beer after the game. And all those aspects were socially strong and aggressive and I guess people perceived it as being aggro. The autographs in the bar were all part of it at that time, which is not right, but you felt as a young player you could do this because senior players were rebelling against administration and against the system, and that is great because we had just finished school and we had rebelled against the school system.'

At school Hookes got bored with class work but loved reading the lore of cricket – less Charles Dickens and more Charles Macartney. So he gobbled up chunks of Chappell's wisdom and the character-driven stories of campaigns won and lost.

'There was no-one to dilute it if you like, and I got sucked in by it. We had Ashley Mallett, Terry Jenner and Jeff Hammond, so we had a strong nucleus of players who were pretty anti-establishment. So we [Rick Darling and Hookes] got caught up in that.'

Conversely, the attitude of Hookes, Cosier and Darling lifted the older players. Mallett had sensed in previous seasons when losing matches that players became selfish – that they were just hoping for enough runs to warrant being selected again. In 1975–76 he saw new blokes eager to play for Australia and the enthusiasm rubbed off.

Being the two kids of the team, Darling and Hookes became close. They had first met in a schoolboys' team and were now playing with and against their childhood idols. Darling agrees that trying to keep up with veteran players wasn't always conducive to playing well.

'Maybe we left too many runs in the bar,' he reflects.

In the first game Hookes played for South Australia he scored 55 against the West Indies. Against New South Wales it was 15 and 35, followed by 53 against Queensland. His ability to score fast at number six, and his pace in the field, were more than valuable assets for South Australia. It was giving the side a sharp edge that would be needed in the next match against Victoria at the MCG.

Despite the resurgence of South Australia under his buccaneer leadership, Ian Chappell was not the king of Australian cricket in December 1975 – it was his brother Greg.

He steered Australia to an eight-wicket win in the first Test against the West Indies on a dodgy Gabba pitch. While others struggled, Greg Chappell mastered the conditions, being the only player to reach three figures – and he did so in both innings. Lillee, Thommo and Gilmour shared eight wickets in the first innings, Jenner and Mallett four in the second. The match ended with the Chappell brothers together unbeaten at the crease – Greg with 109 and Ian on 74.

To top off the joy for the locals, Queensland sat well on top of the Shield table with former New South Wales batsman Ian Davis joining Greg and Thommo as star imports. Queensland's long-held dream of winning a Sheffield Shield grew larger when it thrashed New South Wales at the SCG by 172 runs. Chappell made 124 and Davis 61. Thommo took seven wickets and broke opener Len Richardson's arm.

The photograph in the *Sydney Morning Herald* of Richardson sitting at home on the couch, with his arm in a sling receiving a cup of coffee from his sister, Margaret, was a gentler portrayal of the state of interstate play than the one seen in Melbourne's *Sun News-Pictorial*. In that journal, the headline 'BUMPER WAR' accompanied a photo of Max Walker being stretchered off the WACA.

Western Australian captain Rod Marsh had a simple explanation: they started it. Marsh pointed the finger at Victorian pace bowler Alan Hurst, estimating that in his 21 overs (168 balls) at least 60 balls were short-pitched. A century by all-rounder Trevor Laughlin, and Hurst's fire, had the Victorians leading on the first innings by 38.

Marsh was furious about Hurst targeting tailenders Mick Malone and Bob Paulsen and told Lillee to unleash hell. His 5/58 off 11 overs included a delivery that broke Walker's eye socket. Marsh explained that Walker was a Test batsman who could handle things. The plan was to bounce and then york him. That Lillee never got to the york stage was 'regrettable'.

Umpire Don Hawks asked Marsh to tell his bowlers to settle down, which he did. Victoria was dismissed for 122 and the home side won the match with four wickets in hand.

The Victorians weren't the only ones limping to the MCG for the next Shield match. Ian Chappell had a bad ankle that left him walking like a new-born foal. If the match had been a Test he would have ruled himself out but he believed he could manage a four-day game. He had enjoyed batting for Australia free from the mental stress of being captain but now he resumed the leadership role. To win at the MCG was something he had never experienced in 13 seasons playing for South Australia. The state had only won twice in Melbourne in the past 60 years.

Hookes knew all about the interstate rivalry and would later reflect that the way Victoria approached cricket was based on its football mentality. He said conversations with former players in Melbourne confirmed his suspicion.

'I thought the most childish attacks were from Victoria. They seem to think aggression is [bowling] short and fast and if you hit somebody that is great. Whereas aggression in cricket is getting the bloke out. Simple as that.'

Despite his damaged eye, Walker took the new ball in tandem with Hurst. Captain Ian Redpath set fields with slips and multiple gullies and hoped the unusually green MCG wicket would do the rest.

In came South Australia's openers, Ashley 'Splinter' Woodcock and Rick 'Stumpy' Drewer, who were a contrast in style and temperament.

Woodcock was lean, right-handed and quietly spoken. He was a physical education teacher at St Peter's College and was working toward a PhD. Drewer was stocky, left-handed and possessed a ready, uproarious laugh. He loved music and set up a DJ business to supplement his income, spinning discs at parties he called 'SWORD', an acronym for The Swinging World of Rick Drewer.

While they were the same age, Woodcock had come into the side as a 20-year-old and played a Test match against New Zealand in 1974, while Drewer, 27, was overlooked for years and had all but given up on thoughts of first-class cricket when he was selected.

Their differences melted away when they batted together and because they had been club cricket team mates at university for years they were familiar with each other.

'We were both pretty conservative but we ran singles no-one could believe because we instinctively knew,' recalls Drewer.

'We had Ian and Cosier, then Hookes and Darling, so plenty of people who could score faster. So in my way of thinking it was balanced.'

Their partnership at the MCG was 33 when Woodcock was caught behind. Chappell made only nine before falling to Bright off Laughlin. Cosier came in against his old state and found the wicket placid and the runs plentiful. With his short back lift and powerful hitting, most of his 71 runs came forward of the wicket.

But the longer he was at the crease the more his right leg ached. Cosier had damaged a hamstring in the pre-season and the injury had returned. With restricted movement he started playing more cannily and, in doing so, toyed with left-arm spinner Bright.

'I was giving Bright the shits because I kept playing him down past third slip. I couldn't move much and putting Bright behind point and picking up runs there was great fun.'

Darling made 26. Hookes and Jenner were unbeaten with the score at 253 when the 65 overs expired. Chappell told them to keep batting the remaining six overs until stumps where they finished at 5/279 – Hookes (54) and Jenner (38) both not out.

The busiest person in the South Australian rooms before the second day was the physiotherapist, Barry Richardson. Jenner had strained his back and required time on the massage table to get warmed up while Cosier needed his bad leg strapped. Dennis Yagmich was also gingerly taping up his hands. The wicketkeeper had never broken a digit but the pace of Prior had left deep bruises in his palms and at the base of his fingers.

'Most quick bowlers have deliveries that skid through to you but Fang had so much pace through the air. They would just hit your gloves with a huge thud.'

Most of the thuds early on Saturday came from the bat as Redpath and Paul Hibbert put on 38 in 49 minutes. Redpath had an unusual look at the crease – his cap sat over his jug ears at the end of his long neck that resembled that of a Galapagos tortoise. Chappell deeply admired him and fought to have him included in any XI he captained. He was a counterpoint to the fiery members of the team. Off field he had an interest in antiques and fishing. Sometimes during matches Chappell would notice a faraway look in Redpath's eye and say to Marsh 'He's got a trout on the line'.

His serene approach belied an inner fire. The previous summer the Australian side had been insulted by the comments of board secretary Alan Barnes. It began when Lillee had written in a column how poorly the players were paid. Tim Caldwell from the board told Chappell to 'speak to your fast bowler'. He refused because he agreed with Lillee. Prior to the Test in Sydney, Barnes said the players could take or leave what they were paid because there were 500,000 cricketers who would love to play for Australia for nothing.

Chappell was fuming when he heard about the comments and stormed into the rooms looking for Barnes. Redpath had got there first and had the secretary by the throat up against the wall.

'I thought, "Well, I don't have to make any more points." Better from the mildest man in the team anyway because they would have thought same old Chappell crap, up in the air about something.'

With the Victorian openers in control, Chappell asked Cosier if he could spell Prior and Attenborough. He agreed to try and wobble a few through. His second ball was short and wide. Redpath nicked it and Yagmich threw himself to snag the offering. Cosier remembers the ball starting on middle and leg.

'Redpath swung to try to squeeze it behind square leg and it was the outswinger and he didn't pick it. Lots of things help you win the game but that was a wicket I always remember because he was such a great player.'

Three overs later Cosier limped off. Hibbert continued to 63 and Graham Yallop added 79. An unbeaten 55 from Richie Robinson pushed Victoria within four runs (7/275) of South Australia when Redpath declared. In doing so, he collected five batting points while denying the visitors a chance to gain another bowling point. In the final 23 minutes of the session South Australia added eight runs.

In front of a good Sunday crowd Victoria made South Australia revert to type. Drewer went for ten and Chappell for six. The crowd hooted the captain as he trudged off. Barry Curtin thought Chappell held the honour of being both the most respected man among Australian players and the most booed by crowds.

Aided by a runner, Cosier batted well until he was caught behind for 49. It was the beginning of a collapse – from 3/114 to 177 all out. The only resistance came from Darling and Mallett. The veteran off-spinner had been feeling his age. On Saturday he retired from the field with gastro. Batting with the dashing Darling didn't help his constitution, and when the teenager took off for a quick single, Mallett sent him back. As he whirled around mid-pitch to scramble back, Laughlin threw the ball into Robinson and Darling was run out for 48.

*

When Chappell spoke to the side before the season he hadn't appealed for dominant play. Instead, he asked for regular contributions. He knew he would get them from Jenner and Mallett and was thrilled by Prior. The unknown bowler who shared the new ball was Geoff Attenborough who carried the unflattering nickname 'Scatters'.

It was given to him as a less-than-accurate left-arm seamer at Adelaide Cricket Club by captain Ken Cunningham. Attenborough was 16 at the time and had been playing against men for three years. He liked mucking around in the nets and trying different things. He developed a fast off-break and learnt to swing it both ways.

He was picked for his first state game in 1972–73 but wasn't considered again for two seasons. In 1975–76 he was behind Stan Wilson who was faster but who played only in the game against New South Wales. Once picked, Attenborough became a foil for Fang and belied his nickname.

'He was so tight at the other end,' recalls Prior. 'When the ball got old he came into his own – he was a work horse.'

Chappell came to admire Attenborough's cricket smarts.

'He was one of the first I remember doing this in the fourth innings. He used to come around the wicket and angle into right-handers but cut the ball away. On Adelaide Oval the blokes who rolled their fingers over could get the ball to move off the seam and Scatters was very good at that, and it was his idea.'

There was a blue-collar ethic to the new-ball combination that Attenborough believed helped the team gel.

'We got a start and we got confident and kept going. There weren't many complex people in the team. I was a butcher, Fang was a worker, Ian was captain, TJ was TJ, and Rowdy was funny,' he recalls.

As Fang's reputation grew, Scatters found opportunities in the shadow of his partner's reputation.

'Guys would try to see off Fang and they might have a go at me. I was perhaps faster than they thought because I bowled up around 130.'

So it was against Victoria in the second innings. Redpath mistimed a cut off Attenborough and Drewer caught him in the gully after just six minutes. Robert Baldry came up the order as night watchman, and the Victorians painted the game a shade of beige – adding 17 runs in 65 minutes. Baldry had only ground out six runs in almost an hour when Attenborough trapped him lbw.

At stumps Victoria was 2/17 with a full day to score the 165 needed.

Despite being low on energy Mallett knew much of the final day's fate would be in his hands. Cosier was ruled out and Chappell often used Mallett to hold up an end in the final innings. He was far from the Victorian crowd favourite as he jogged onto the MCG. On the Saturday he and his captain had attracted public ire over an appeal against Yallop. The Victorian left-hander had tried to sweep a well-pitched delivery from Mallett. Drewer, who was fielding at short-leg, feared the worst and dived for cover. However, Yallop only got a top edge and the ball floated straight up. Yagmich tried to get around Yallop to catch the ball but in the tussle Yallop lost his feet and fell to the ground with the South Australian wicketkeeper on top of him.

Mallett and Chappell appealed to umpire Jack Collins for obstructing the field. It was turned down. At tea the South Australians headed for their rooms when two women shouted at Chappell that he was the captain of a team of bad sports. He dismissed them with two fingers, which prompted a mouthful of abuse from another spectator.

Mallett broke through early, clean bowling Stillman for four, and when Hibbert tried to hook Attenborough and was brilliantly caught at square leg by Drewer, Victoria was listing at 4/46 needing 135 to win.

Five minutes before lunch Mallett had Laughlin caught behind for 17 with the total at 5/78, but in the afternoon session the home state took control. Yallop and Robinson steered the ship gently towards another outright win over the angry red-topped bull ants from across the border. Their 60-run partnership came in 79 minutes and ended when Robinson misjudged a ball from Mallett that kept low.

Twenty minutes later Yallop reluctantly left the crease after being caught close to the wicket by Drewer off Mallett for 62.

Victoria needed 34 to win with three wickets in hand. Walker and Bright looked steady against Mallett and Jenner and were unbeaten at tea. Victoria needed only 13 runs.

During the break Chappell knew his only option was the shock tactic. When play resumed in the final session he took the ball off Jenner and handed it to Fang.

He handed it back.

'I said to Ian, "This ball is out of shape, can we change it?" He said, "Nah, nah, it will bounce odd or skid along so keep it." That worked out alright.'

His first ball hit Bright's pad, plum in front, on the half volley. Two balls later a full toss shattered the stumps behind Leigh Baker. The South Australians watched Hurst walk slowly to join Walker at the crease. Fang reared one in and Hurst scrambled a single – 12 to win. Walker flicked two off the next ball – ten to win.

The Victorians took three off Mallett's over allowing Walker to face Prior with seven needed. The first ball of his second over screamed through the air and knocked off peg from its footing. As Jack Collins gathered the bails and uprooted the remaining stumps, the South Australians surged into a delirious pack around their fast bowler. As Chappell saw it, in the games against New South Wales and Victoria Fang had bowled 12 balls that had taken six wickets for three runs and resulted in 20 points for South Australia.

The victory for Chappell was bittersweet. He believed it was the worst Shield game he had ever played, failing with the bat twice and dropping two vital catches. But he couldn't remember enjoying a victory like it for some time. Redpath blamed himself for the loss because he contributed so few runs.

South Australia was now within reach of Queensland at the top of the Shield table and the belief was visceral. The captain rejected the idea that luck was playing a part. Instead he saw determination, hard work and 'an overwhelming will to keep pushing forward for a win'. He felt that, as captain, he had to do everything he could for his players because he was getting everything from them that they had. The players celebrated the win over their nemesis long and hard and, without articulating it, felt they would and could run through brick walls for Chappell. Their devotion to him was at odds with the administrators for whom he was becoming an increasingly isolated and cantankerous figure. Chappell had again been reported by the umpires for abusive language, only this time the SACA referred the matter to the ACB.

CHAPTER FIVE

ON THE OFFENSIVE

The first incarnation of the Chappell Stand at the Adelaide Oval opened before Christmas in 2003. The three brothers, along with their mother, Jeanne, were feted during the lunch break on the first day of the Ashes Test. They unveiled the stand on the eastern side – fittingly, next to the Victor Richardson Gates. Ian said he liked the stand being near the hill, which was home to the knowledgeable larrikin supporter, but he added that he would have remained happy just with the bar.

The Chappell Bar was under the Members Stand and featured two large photographs of Ian and Greg in full flight. Dennis Lillee admired them a few months later when he was preparing for an interview with Kerry O'Brien that I was producing for the ABC.

'Ian Chappell, I called him "the butcher" when he batted because he was cruel on bowlers. But Greg Chappell was an artist,' said Lillee. 'You can't think of anyone better than him, maybe Tendulkar is and maybe Lara is, but I don't think so.'

If O'Brien had been a cricketer he would have been akin to Bill 'Tiger' O'Reilly – a ginger-headed Irishman who bowled leggies and never let a significant question go unasked. He pushed Lillee to compare the brothers as captains.

'I didn't like Greg's approach to the way he captained. I guess I was spoilt by Ian Chappell.'

Lillee's explanation was that while Greg was like a schoolteacher wagging his finger, his brother would sit down after a day's play, gradually talk about things and make it seem like the bowler's idea that Lillee would do something different next time.

Greg was a perfectionist who expected perfection from others and was frustrated when it didn't come. Rod Marsh tells a story about a series of dropped catches in a Test in Brisbane. When the first went down in the slips Greg groaned, and when the second went down he growled. Then when Marsh grassed a nick he feared a blast from his captain but Greg turned to the other fieldsmen and roared, 'Now you've got him dropping them.'

When Dennis Yagmich went for a catch for South Australia and it fell to the turf he looked across at Ian Chappell at first slip and apologised.

'I just said, "I am so sorry, Ian" because you never wanted to let him down and he just said, "Yag, no-one ever tries to drop a catch." That was the end of it.'

Ashley Mallett believes Ian understood empowerment before it was a management buzzword.

'You could set your own field and he would listen to suggestions. If it was ridiculous he would say, "Maybe one day we will try [that]." He wouldn't instruct you how to bowl, ever. He might just say, "We need a wicket."'

Chappell believed being captain was not just a job from eleven in the morning until six at night. He rated respect as the most important thing for a captain to have attained, and he applauded the Australian system whereby the captain was selected from the team rather than, as in the English system, being named by a selection committee ahead of being given a side.

'That way the captain has earned respect from other players as a player. Then he can earn respect as a leader. There are two parts: captaincy and leadership,' says Chappell.

'Any cricketer can pin up the batting order, change the bowlers and move the fielders around. That doesn't take a lot of cricket knowledge. The important part is leadership and that is where you spend time outside the cricketing hours with your players, and the time you invest there you will reap the rewards on the field.'

This is where a third part comes in: humanity. Chappell often refers to the value of a human being. It is how he describes one of his great inspirations, Sir Garfield Sobers. He likes to shock people awake by telling them that as a teenager he replaced Sobers in the South Australian team. He is being a smart alec but it is true.

After the enchanting 1960–61 West Indies tour of Australia, state cricket was energised when several players returned the following summer to play in the Shield competition. Wes Hall played for Queensland, Rohan Kanhai for Western Australia and Sobers for South Australia. While Hall led all bowlers with 43 wickets and Kanhai averaged 44 with the bat, Sobers did it all. He was a powerful batsman, a brilliant bowler of both pace and spin and an extraordinary fieldsman.

His place in the game was forcefully announced years later in the lounge room of Keith Miller. Australia's greatest all-rounder was watching a Test match on television when the commentator described his old captain Bradman as the greatest cricketer of all time.

'Wrong,' declared Miller. 'The greatest batsman of all time was Don Bradman but the greatest cricketer of all time was Garry Sobers.'

When Sobers first came into the West Indies side as a teenager, Miller took a shine to him. Miller and Ray Lindwall were the Lillee–Thomson of the 1955 tour of the Caribbean in which Australia went unbeaten. They wreaked havoc with their bowling. One evening they knocked on the door of the hotel room being shared by Sobers and Collie Smith. They demanded the two young men join them for a drink to talk cricket.

Miller understood the mind game of cricket and how it is more testing than the physical aspects of the sport. He would later write of his admiration for the Caribbean approach.

'Of all the nations who play cricket, the West Indians show a bigger desire to play cricket joyfully than any other race. It is in their minds. They also possess a natural ability to relax, which is one of the foundations of good batting.'

At the end of the tour Miller gave Sobers his bat in an act of encouragement and a sign of respect. The feeling was mutual. Sobers came away from that series with a deep admiration for Australian cricket, believing the tourists were the closest to the West Indies in their approach to the game.

His opinion seemed justified by the 1960–61 West Indies tour of Australia. During that series Bradman encouraged the tourists to consider playing Sheffield Shield cricket.

Sobers's friendship with Bradman grew. He and his wife and newborn son dined at Bradman's home and enjoyed long talks at the oval. Sobers grew bored watching cricket and retreated to the back of the room to lie down. That is where Bradman would find him, especially when he needed runs for South Australia. He almost made personal pleas for big scores and Sobers delighted in delivering them to him. The other, albeit less regal, presence in the rooms was Chappell.

'I played with Ian as a young man and saw him in the South Australian dressing room even before he played for South Australia,' recalls Sobers. 'He used to come in and listen for hours and hours to the fellows talk about the game. He was always a student of the game and was the type of person who was always going to be a good captain.'

Chappell's first game for South Australia was against New South Wales in Sydney. He was 12th man. Against the attack of Alan Davidson and Richie Benaud, Sobers scored 251 in the second innings and took nine wickets as South Australia won by 132 runs.

He then flew back to the Caribbean for Test duties. In came Chappell.

By the time Sobers returned for his second season in Adelaide, Chappell was still in the side. But he was struggling and when Victorian Ian Meckiff conspired to get him out for one and none at the MCG Chappell went to Sobers.

Over a beer Sobers explained how he played back and across like Chappell but took his guard from leg-, not middle-, stump. He suggested this technical change might help. Chappell acted on it and it did work. Along with the batting masterclass, however, he remembers the humanity.

'It always stuck in my mind that here was a bloke just assuming the mantle as the best all-round cricketer in the world and he treated an 18-year-old as an equal. Just batting down the other end would have been enough but that he treated me as an equal meant a lot.'

Chappell and Sobers played under Captain Les Favell, a stocky and adventurous opening batsman who left Sydney for Adelaide in search of opportunities. Favell urged his players to entertain those who had paid to come and watch.

'Les was a very aggressive captain. I was lucky being a number three batsmen because you can show your intent, that you intend getting on with things as soon as you can. That rubs off,' says Chappell.

'It was the same with Les who opened the batting. He actually said to us if we batted first he wanted 300 in a day, and if we were 8/300 Les was happy, but if we were 2/270 Les had the shits and he would let us know.

'I had the impression there was a feeling of inferiority in South Australia until Les took over as captain. Les didn't feel he was inferior to anybody and Garry Sobers confirmed that in the way he played.'

Sobers loved that approach. In his eyes the best captains were always looking for how to win while the worst were the ones who 'give you the time of day and little else'.

Declarations were part of it. Sobers bristled when captains pushed the other side out of the game and he noticed how crowds fell away when it happened. Chappell believed that by showing the opposition from the first ball that he was trying to win the game he put pressure on defensive captains. His opening statement was that one of only two things will happen: we will win or we will lose. A draw, he figured, shouldn't be in the equation.

South Australia won the Sheffield Shield in 1963–64 with Sobers in full cry. That year South Africa toured Australia and when they played South Australia, Sobers asked Favell if he could bat wearing his West Indian cap, rather than the state one, to shove it up the visitors. By the end of the 1960s the global move against apartheid led to the 1970–71 South African tour of Australia being called off.

Bradman pulled strings to arrange a world XI to fill the void, and he twisted Sobers's arm to captain the team. Sobers was already coming to Adelaide for another season of Shield cricket and was therefore available. The series also gave Bradman a chance to see how Chappell would go as captain and, in particular, how his raw paceman, Lillee, would perform. And all this would be a prologue for the 1972 Ashes tour.

Sobers was among those Lillee put a spear through when he announced his arrival in Perth, and Chappell's leadership grew from the experience of facing the best in the world. The series ended 2–1 to the tourists and was played amid mutual admiration.

Alongside Lillee's bowling, the standout performance was Sobers's 254 in Melbourne, an innings Bradman said was 'probably the greatest exhibition of batting ever seen in Australia'.

Chappell used eight bowlers to try to stem the flow. Eventually Greg Chappell had Sobers caught by Doug Walters. Among the others who toiled was leg-spinner Terry Jenner. Although he finished the innings with 4/87 off 20 overs, his role as cannon fodder for Sobers was repeated over and over thanks to video footage of Sobers's knock that was distributed to clubs.

Bradman believed the footage should be shown as an instructional tool all around Australia and he even agreed to provide the narration. As a representative of Coca-Cola, Jenner found himself popular at functions where he would introduce the film. He then sat embarrassed at the back of a darkened room with a shaft of light from the projector replaying his bowling nightmare, set to the disembodied, tuneless voice of the Don:

Jenner once more, and this time it is a full toss outside off stump and Sobers plays it absolutely perfectly through the cover field. Now here is a repeat of the same shot, a full toss outside off stump and bang through the cover. Sobers hasn't even moved … and here it is in slow motion, a perfect example of how to play a cover drive. Admittedly it is a full toss but it is so beautifully executed ... Jenner again, this time a little short of a length and Sobers pulls it around to the on-side ....

If ever there was a bowler who didn't need reminding of failure, even in the face of batting genius, it was Jenner. Known as 'TJ' he was a bearish figure with a big voice and a boisterous manner. He was known for yapping on the field and would later regret some of his more graphic behaviour.

As a leg-spinner he didn't have a short, sharp one to square things up with a batsman. Instead his craft relied on bounce and lift, and luring the batsman into playing or, hopefully, misplaying a shot. Someone who stayed at home in the crease was no good to Jenner, he needed them to come out and the act of doing so he called 'tossing out the burley'. It was a game that was played on the edge because there was always a chance he would be savaged. Favell told him he had 25 runs to play with between wickets and he needed them. When it went badly it was a lonely place to be and he said sometimes all he had left was his sense of humour.

He had learnt to play at Corrigin in the Western Australian wheat belt about three hours from Perth. He came to town to play and at 19 was picked for the state as a leg-spinning all-rounder. The trouble was that the West had other spinners in Tony Lock and Tony Mann. There was also an off-spinner in the wings: Ashley Mallett.

Jenner and Mallett first met as teenagers at the Mount Lawley Cricket Club. They contrasted in almost every way. Where Jenner was loud, Mallett was quiet. Jenner laughed heartily while Mallett cracked dry gags. If Jenner was built like a woodchopper at the

Royal Perth Show, Mallett appeared more ready for lawn bowls. But they shared a love of the game and a fascination with the spinning ball. After playing grade cricket on Saturday they would head 200 kilometres north of Perth to play Sunday cricket in the town of Miling.

Jenner played sporadically for Western Australia. In his first game he received what he considered a cutting sledge from New South Wales captain Richie Benaud. The match was in Sydney and Western Australia was 5/249 when Jenner came to the crease. Benaud, a master of leg-spin, had been Jenner's idol. As the debutante approached the wicket, Benaud sidled over.

'Oh hello, Terry,' he said cordially, as if they were old mates catching up.

Jenner was speechless but inside a voice said, 'Oh God, he knows my name!' The moment highlighted his feelings of not belonging in this company and he was soon out for two.

While Jenner's appearances were patchy he was at least in the XI. The best Mallett could get was 12th man. He was in that role in a match against South Australia in Perth when Barry Shepherd gave TJ a bowl. Favell was at the crease and his eyes lit up like halogen lamps at the sight of the young leggy.

As he came in to bowl the South Australian captain started singing: 'Happy birthday to me.' He charged down the track and belted the ball to the boundary. The second ball went the same way but was fielded near the fence. Non-striker Chappell took off for a run only to find Favell sending him back and saying, 'Piss off, Chappell, it's my birthday, not yours.'

The lack of opportunity saw both bowlers move to South Australia and develop into regular first-class players but as Mallett became Australia's first choice spinner TJ struggled. His private life could be chaotic and the sport offered a rare chance for public self-esteem.

'I was so pleased just to be part of it. With my personality I think if I had been a regular I would have had an opinion on everything. Just getting a cheque in those days saved me from getting a car repossessed. I was living day to day.'

If cricket was a safe haven then Chappell was his rock. On the field Jenner believed Chappell was always one step ahead of the game with field placings and bowling changes. He never let things drift. There was always a reason for doing things that he could explain logically. Chappell spoke to him as an equal and listened to Jenner's insecurities about bowling. Chappell also bowled leggies and understood the perils of cricket's confidence trick.

On a train going to Melbourne in 1970, Jenner took Chappell away from his card game. The long journeys were spent fraternising, with Chappell acting as social secretary. Each player had to show him the longneck bottles they had brought to share before he was allowed to board the train. Jenner wanted to be serious this time because he had thought of a way to get Ian Redpath out. Chappell was all ears.

When Victoria batted, the captain arranged things as Jenner suggested. He looped one in and Redpath sent a screaming catch to Greg Chappell in cover and was out for 17. Jenner finished with four wickets in each innings; the train back to Adelaide was a night of celebration for him. When the 'Overland' pulled into Murray Bridge around dawn, a conductor slid a copy of the *Advertiser* under the cabin door. In the pale early light Jenner had to brush away tears when he read he had been picked for Australia. He was 26 years old.

*

Jenner was closing in on his 50th birthday when we met one Friday evening in an Adelaide sports bar. He announced his arrival by pointing at the beer tap saying, 'I will have one of those', and then at the bank of betting screens – 'and *not* any of those'.

He was several years out of jail and his reputation as a coach was growing on the back of his work with Shane Warne. His daughter, Trudianne, was with him that weekend and he tenderly made sure she was happy before starting the interview. He mostly spoke about Warne who was becoming the leggy everyone wanted him to be. His self-confidence was evident in his stalking walk to the crease that preceded his muscular ripping of any number of variations.

'He turns the ball more in one session than I did in a season.'

Jenner related to Warne's roguish nature and became his mystic tutor. In the nets before a Test match in Adelaide, TJ would set up with Warne, light up a stogie and talk about bowling, like astronomers discussing the orbits of the night sky.

Warne's climb from prodigy to master was well documented. On the eve of his breaking Lillee's test record of 355 wickets the

ABC dispatched me to interview Jenner. He provided fascinating insights. When Warne got to 500 we repeated the performance. When Warne was on 699, and nearing the end, Jenner rang: 'Should we do it one more time?'

Each time he seemed more self-assured. Two cricket magazines in the UK asked me about writing a profile on his rehabilitation but Jenner declined. He was starting to understand the power of his own story and needed to protect its value.

It was far from the man sitting in a back corner of a sports bar that night several years earlier. Then he was at his nadir. He had punted while playing and drank heavily. After cricket ended the two habits collided and his debts became insurmountable. He was working in car sales and stole money from his boss to pay the bookies. When it caught up with him he was slotted for six-and-a-half years. Arriving at Yatala Prison the warden said to him: 'You will find out who your fucking friends are now, Jenner.'

Chappell visited. A television camera followed and he didn't flinch. It was one of his boys. They had shared what Jenner considers one of the defining moments of Chappell's captaincy in the West Indies in 1973. That was the tour where they lost Lillee and Massie. Jenner says the feeling in the group was that everyone had to do their bit. His best was 5/90 in the drawn fifth Test at Port of Spain which included the wickets of Roy Fredericks, Alvin Kallicharran and Rohan Kanhai.

The defining moment came earlier in the third Test at Trinidad. Jenner says Chappell was always positive in team meetings but the Australians were grumpy at lunch on the final day. They had reason to be; the West Indies were 4/268 needing 66 to win with Kallicharran on 91. Chappell didn't feel like eating and instead lay on a bench and put his cap over his eyes. For the first time since taking over as captain he heard the players grizzling. Among them was Jenner.

'I was personally disappointed in how I bowled. I had taken four wickets in the first innings. I come back to this feeling of belonging because I felt in the second innings there would be more turn and a great chance for me and I am sure Kerry O'Keeffe felt the same. He bowled well, got four, and I got none.

'I was in the dumps at lunch and most figured with Kallicharran playing so well the game was over. Ian gave us a fair spray. One of few times he ever did. It was hot and oppressive and everyone was tired but he didn't accept the game was over, and the good news is neither did Maxie [Walker]. The ball had sheets of skin hanging off it. He put some saliva on it and reckoned he could get it to swing. The first one did – I heard the nick from fine-leg. Rod Marsh took the catch and threw the ball in the air and as I ran up from fine-leg it almost landed on me – that is how excited he was. And he said, "Now we have got them."'

They had. From 4/268 the home side was all out for 289 and Australia had secured a 44-run victory.

Jenner replayed the episode to me in full cry with arms waving and sound effects. After it was over he seemed deflated and sat back in the semi-darkness. He looked at his daughter and started talking about his mistakes in life, and his responsibilities to her and to Warne. He became emotional. Did he have any advice for Warne who seemed to have some of the excesses of his mentor?

'The same advice Ian Chappell gave me: you have got to know yourself.'

*

After the win at the MCG, the South Australians flew home with over a month until their next Shield match. On the plane team manager Cec Starr carried in his pocket the report the umpires, Jack Collins and Kevin Carmody, had filed about Chappell's behaviour and language on the field.

It began as a result of one of Chappell's dropped catches. He was hooted by the Victorian crowd and it sparked some wordplay and banter. This wasn't unusual. One spectator had enough volume for Chappell to hear him bellow 'Get a bag!'

Chappell shouted back, 'I should have used your mouth – it is big enough.'

The crowd roared back and continued pecking away at him. Team mates had seen this before, even when Chappell had pretended to fumble a ball in the field just to toy with spectators. They saw him laughing.

Collins moved away from the wicket and waved his arms across his body, semaphoring for the pantomime to stop and mouthing the words 'that is enough'. Chappell signalled for Collins to resume his position behind the stumps. At the end of the over, as Chappell passed Carmody, the pair exchanged words and then Collins spoke to him. Whatever occurred in those conversations was written into the report sitting in Starr's pocket along with mentions of the behaviour of Jenner and Laughlin. Copies had already been sent by priority mail to the ACB.

The perspective of the umpires differs from Ashley Woodcock's, which is why he says Chappell was misunderstood by outsiders. Woodcock has a clear recollection of the events which he says were designed to protect Jenner.

'TJ had been bowling poorly, losing his confidence and the crowd was getting on him when he was fielding. So Ian started having a crack at them and so they quickly turned on him. It was about diverting attention onto him and away from TJ. That is why he was such a great leader; he always had the player's back.'

Chappell arrived in Adelaide wearing white shoes, white jeans and a white denim jacket over a patterned body shirt. He was carrying an almost human-sized stuffed Womble which was a gift for his daughter, Amanda, who had arrived with her mother, Kay, to collect him. He was dismissive and defiant when asked by Mike Coward about being reported. He didn't think he was guilty of offensive behaviour and he didn't think the umpires should have intervened in the chiacking. It wasn't any of their business and so he wasn't going to apologise.

That he took this stand is significant given what occurred in the visitors' rooms directly after the palpitating win over Victoria. As the South Australians celebrated, two Australian Cricket Board members, Ray Steele and chairman Bob Parish, came in to talk to Chappell. They were aware of the report and offered him a way out. If he apologised to the umpires, they said, then all would be forgotten. He refused on the basis that he said what he said and if that led to a report then he should face the charges. His family had never sanctioned abusing umpires and Chappell intended telling the administrators honestly what he said, and if he was guilty then he should be suspended rather than tacitly admit to something to make it go away. The threat of suspension this time didn't concern him as much as the welfare of his players.

'I don't have any loyalty to the SACA anymore but I am loyal to the SA players who are trying so desperately hard at the moment to win the Shield,' he told Coward at the airport.

As he headed out of the terminal with the giant Womble under his arm he acknowledged two taxi drivers who shouted out from the rank.

'Good on you, Ian ... tell them to go to hell.'

The consequences were clear, however. With the threat from the SACA after the New South Wales game that further reports would result in punishment, Chappell could be suspended for Shield matches. Word soon came that the ACB wanted Chappell to front a disciplinary tribunal – but not until after the second Test against the West Indies at the WACA.

Chappell had one night at home before returning to the airport to fly to Perth.

CHAPTER SIX

'REPREHENSIBLE' BEHAVIOUR

Cricket at the WACA is played with the volume turned up loud. The most isolated outpost of the English game is where the contest on a bouncing, rock-hard deck favours the brave and exposes the weak. The angry sun that bakes the ground creates inland heat that draws cool air off the Indian Ocean in the afternoon. While this relief, known as the 'Fremantle Doctor', soothes spectators it also provides a corridor of extra pace for bowlers.

When Andy Roberts's second ball cannoned into Rick McCosker's pad the five West Indians in the slip cordon flew up as one. For the second Test, Clive Lloyd had picked four fast bowlers in his team for the first time and its success began a strategy that would continue for the next 25 years.

The pace attack accounted for 19 of the 20 Australian wickets, with Roberts responsible for nine of them. The tourists won by an innings and 87 runs. The match featured two memorable batting performances – one from Roy Fredericks and the other from Ian Chappell.

Chappell emerged from the rooms blinking up at the sun after McCosker was out. The West Indies put a man at deep fine-leg and bounced him, hoping for a hook shot. He disappointed them. He lost Alan Turner with the score at 23 and then his brother Greg at 70. Just before lunch he mistimed a delivery from Keith Boyce that hammered into the inside of his knee. The excruciating blow added to his ankle woes and he limped off to the break with 3/88 on the board.

Redpath, Marsh, Gilmour and Walker all came and went as Chappell continued. With the 'Doctor' blowing and the sun heading toward Africa he fought on, scoring his 14th Test century and 5000th Test run. In the final over of the day he provided the only chance, hooking Roberts, but was dropped by the exhausted fielder at deep backward-leg. At stumps he was unconquered on 148 having batted for 365 minutes. Keith Butler from the *Advertiser* wondered if Chappell had ever played a more responsible innings.

Chappell's innings was put together after his collision with authority and the resulting consequences of that. His behaviour against Victoria was the subject of a phone hook-up between members of the ACB Umpires' Appointments Committee which included ACB chairman Bob Parish and representatives from South Australia, Queensland and Western Australia.

As a result, the night before the game, the ACB handed him a severe reprimand and threatened him with suspension. The reprimand was for abusing the umpires. In later years it would be one of Chappell's few regrets from cricket; not that he had been sanctioned but that he had abused an umpire.

After the announcement was relayed to Perth, Parish sat back in his office chair in Melbourne and answered questions from an ABC journalist about Chappell:

'How would you describe his behaviour?'

'Reprehensible is the word I used and I believe that is the right word.'

'Why was he only reprimanded?'

'I think I made that perfectly clear in my statement, and in the board's statement, that because of his contribution to Australian cricket, which is quite remarkable, the board decided that it would severely reprimand him.'

'Mr Parish, what do you think is more important – the players of the game or the officials?'

'That is easily answered. The game is more important than both. I believe that everybody has to realise that the game of cricket, which is a big game in this country, a national game, has to be administered. The administrators do the very best they can in the interests of the game as a whole. The player has got to accept that and realise that the game is not put on for his personal benefit.'

'It is a very emotional game now, isn't it?'

'It can be emotional. I think any game of any quality is emotional but you have got to, as a player, be able to control your emotions.'

The punishment was seen in some quarters as benign. Victorian coach Frank Tyson raged against Chappell's behaviour in his account of the summer:

'I questioned whether Chappell had ever paused to consider the antipathy he was stirring up in the breasts of umpires throughout the length and breadth of the Test and Sheffield Shield arena. It seemed that the ex-Australian captain was hell-bent on martyrdom in order to raise a plaintiff cry of "look how cruelly the administrators are treating the players again".

'He rescued Australia from the plight of a disastrous beginning and by scoring a face-saving century on the first day of the game could almost be seen as thumbing his nose at the administrators and daring them to omit him from the side.'

Chappell's contribution to Australian cricket continued on the second day at the WACA until Michael Holding slipped one through his defence when he was on 156.

The 329 first innings total looked reasonable with Lillee and Thommo working on a strip that already had cracks appearing, but Fredericks got ahead of them blasting 169 off 145 balls, a knock that included 27 fours and a six. It was batting in the raw. Lloyd's 149 off 186 later seemed pedestrian.

Jenner watched much of it from the rooms. He was 12th man for the Test match and in that role completed a soul-draining hat-trick. This was the third time he had been included in a Test squad in his home state, and each time he had been relegated to running the drinks and folding the towels.

Midway through Fredericks's mighty knock, Greg Chappell

called Jenner onto the ground as a substitute fieldsman. Jenner thought this was another indignity because if he was involved in a wicket then he wouldn't even be credited with it. Instead the card would read 'SUB fielder', not 'Jenner'.

What he saw, though, was a force of nature with a stick of willow in his hand.

'I went to cover point and Lillee bowls and then *bang*, I hear this noise and the ball just comes off Fredo's bat toward me and before I can even move it curls in the air past me like a rocket and smashes into the fence.'

The tourists' 585 gave them a 256-run cushion. Greg Chappell was the highest-scoring Australian with 43 in the second innings. Roberts took 7/54. The series sat at 1–1.

*

Fredericks had, by himself, equalled the entire Australian second innings score and so was named the Man of the Match, a title which came with a $300 cheque from Benson & Hedges. The tradition of the day suggested that the cash was divided among his team mates. Tobacco sponsorship was increasing and formed a significant part of the money the players earned. In 1975–76 the Australians received $400 per day for a Test match. It was topped up by a bonus of $400 per Test match and $450 for expenses. Each player also took a $1625 slice of the Benson and Hedges money, with $1200 put into a benevolent fund if he played in all six Test matches. The superannuation only applied to those who had played more than 20 Tests. There was also a division of Man of the Match prize money.

All totalled, a player such as Ian Chappell, who played in a full Shield (eight games) and Test (six games) series, could earn about $10,000 for the summer. The average full-time earning for an Australian worker in 1976 was $9,396.

The Perth Test had drawn almost 66,000 spectators, which was a few hundred more than the Brisbane match – the two smallest crowds of the summer. Still, the game at the WACA had taken $140,354 at the gate alone. The third Test at the MCG starting on Boxing Day would attract 222,755 in just four days and take $310, 230.

Chappell was better off financially than most cricketers, and not just because he was selected for every match. He had been in the smokes game himself, working in sales for WD & HO Wills, which afforded him time off to play. After returning from the West Indies in 1973 he set himself up as his own company – Ian Chappell Enterprises. Along with match payments he earned money from personal sponsorships, promotions, writing columns, speaking engagements and golf days. He had a deal to wear Adidas shoes, which had caused strife in Brisbane because clothing brands contravened ACB rules for player conduct.

The economics of Australian cricket was structured around Test matches and the success generated by Chappell's teams had swollen coffers. Amid the success those inside the game struggled to see the opportunity sitting under their noses. One-day cricket had been part of the fixtures of state cricket since 1969–70 with a knockout cup competition that included New Zealand. The Kiwis took the inaugural trophy beating Victoria in the final at the MCG. In 1975–76, New Zealand withdrew from the competition – which would be won by Queensland.

The English pioneered the format with a county one-day knockout tournament in 1963. The first international one-day match had only come about because filthy January weather in Melbourne had washed out the third Ashes Test in 1971. The two countries agreed to a game along the lines of a county limited-overs match. More than twice as many spectators (46,006) turned up as expected, paying almost $34,000 for a look at what many believed was a gimmick game.

By the mid-1970s the gimmick tag hadn't really worn off, despite the growing interest in the format. The administrators scheduled only one limited-overs match on the next MCC tour of Australia in 1975, despite the inaugural World Cup looming in England later that year. The tournament was a success with the drama generated by exciting group and knockout games being capped by the thrilling final at Lord's between Australia and the West Indies. The game itself was played like a mini Test match – the players wore white, the ball was red and Chappell set a field with three slips and two gullies for his quicks.

The Australians lost that final but had an opportunity for revenge when the same teams faced each other in a limited-overs match at the Adelaide Oval, two days after the end of the second Test in Perth. The establishment still sniffed at it – believing it an inferior version of 'real' cricket. Frank Tyson thumbed through his dictionary and described the game as 'ersatz'.

There was nothing inauthentic about the baggy green cap that Gary Cosier plonked on top of his bush of red hair. He did his best Cheshire cat impersonation for a photographer in front of the old scoreboard after finding out he had been picked for the one-day game.

'It is a size 7 ½ but don't say I have got a big head,' he quipped 'It's just I have got plenty of hair.'

His first-up century against the tourists that summer had caught the selectors' attention, and his big hitting in Shield games (average 53.6) since hadn't hurt either. The cap brought with it confirmation of Cosier's need to break away. He had stalled in Victoria, and shifting to South Australia had freed him up. In 18 months he had gone from club cricketer to the Australian first XI. His parents, brothers, sister and a cohort of mates from Northcote Cricket Club flew over for the match. They were part of a modest crowd of 14,168.

Greg Chappell sent the tourists in, which suited Gordon Greenidge. The opener had struggled on tour and had been dropped for the second Test after making a pair in the first. Like Viv Richards – who had scored just 24 from three innings – the tour was exposing him. Richards would soon seek the services of sports psychologist Rudi Webster to try to make sense of it all.

Greenidge hammered two sixes and a four as he and Fredericks gathered 33 off Lillee and Gilmour's first four overs. When Cosier was given the ball, Greenidge was in a murderous mood. The first offering was slashed over the cover fence. As he watched the cherry disappear into the crowd, Cosier thought, 'This is a nice start to my first game for Australia – whacked for six'.

For the next delivery Greenidge charged down the wicket and swung mightily with the ball destined to go over the longest boundary in Australia, straight over the sightscreen. The pace of Cosier was not quite that of Lillee or Gilmour and so Greenidge was already part way through the shot when he connected. As a result, the ball lifted straight up. It went so high the spectators in the grandstand couldn't see it and the players in the rooms were wondering where it was.

Cosier stood mid-pitch watching the red pin prick in the sky for so long that Marsh had time to join him. Together they watched. Eventually it began to grow in size as it fell to earth, at which point Marsh backed away and told Cosier the catch was his. With his heart racing and the crowd anticipating, the ball landed in Cosier's palms. He cupped his hands around it, dropped to his knees and bowed his head. Greenidge, caught and bowled Cosier, 41.

'It wasn't really like a [classic] caught and bowled but that is how it went into the card.'

Richards made 74 as the West Indies finished just short of their 40 overs at 224. As in Perth, McCosker was out in Roberts's first over and Chappell came in and did the business. His 63 included eight fours and two enormous sixes over square-leg off consecutive deliveries from Vanburn Holder.

As Australia overhauled the West Indies' total with 67 balls remaining, Tuner made 46 and Greg Chappell 59, while Redpath

(24) and Cosier (25) were unbeaten at the end.

The selectors were happy with their work and that night announced Cosier was in the 12 for the Boxing Day Test in Melbourne. The player who made way for him was Terry Jenner.

After the one-off limited-overs game the West Indies were back at the Adelaide Oval the next day for the start of a three-day game against South Australia. Ashley Woodcock captained the side as Chappell was given the game off. His place was taken by a man who believed cricket should be played like football.

*

In the late 1950s and early 1960s Port Adelaide dominated South Australian football. At one stage the club set an Australian record with six premierships on end. That they also won the reserves' competition five times during that run indicates the width and depth of the club. One of the teams regularly on the wrong end of Port's success was West Adelaide. This was the club of the west end of the city where Harold Chappell ran a pharmacy. He served on the West Adelaide committee and his son Martin and grandsons all followed the club and watched it lose heartbreaking grand finals to Port Adelaide.

'They [Port] were just big, arrogant and strong ... That is how they always have been,' says Barry Curtin. 'It was 75 steps from the sleep-out at my house to Alberton Oval. The us-and-them ethos of the footy club naturally flowed down into the cricket club.'

The cricketers also played with a geographic pride. In the 1960s two barrel-chested athletes emerged who both would complete a rare double of playing football and cricket at the highest level. Neil 'Hawkeye' Hawke and Eric 'Fritz' Freeman both played at full-forward in winter and took the new ball in summer. In the fourth Test against India in Sydney in 1968 they opened the bowling for Australia. This was the first occasion in Australian Test history where two players from the same club had done so.

For all that, there was sometimes a suspicion from Chappell that being from Port Adelaide left players vulnerable.

'When Freeman walked out to bat Les Favell would say, "Get your head down, Fritz" because he couldn't help himself and liked to have a thrash, and often not sensibly. There was one supporter who used to see him coming and would yell out "Carn the Magpies" just as he set foot through the gates onto the oval and that was the end of Fritz's brain. [It was as if] he was playing in a grand final for Port Adelaide and whoosh bang he was out.'

One of the Magpies' creeds was that if you weren't with them then you were against them. Port Adelaide sits geographically down a peninsula from the rest of Adelaide and the isolation feeds into its mind set. There were four Curtin brothers growing up in neighbouring Woodville in the 1950s when the eldest, David, showed promise as a footballer. The clubs were arranged on strict metropolitan zones and talent was guarded zealously. He was zoned to Woodville. Port Adelaide saw a clan they wanted and so arranged for the entire family of six to move house to be within its catchment. Barry Curtin recalls that it happened within a matter of weeks.

The boys eventually showed more promise as cricketers than footballers and three of them would play for South Australia. Even there you never forgot where you came from.

'Barry Curtin was Port Adelaide,' says Cosier. 'He wore whites, not creams [and] he unbuttoned his shirt as far down as possible. He was rough as guts, drank, smoked, hooked, cut – the funniest bloke and a genuine, genuine person. He was carefree and took the piss out of everyone but you always knew you would get the maximum out of Barry.'

Curtin wasn't a regular selection for South Australia but when he had a chance he took it – and there was no thought of self-preservation. He was an extrovert, a natural storyteller and he played life for everything it had. He loved rooming with Wayne Prior because Fang was organised and would arrange the breakfast order that Curtin forgot after a chaotic night. He adored playing for Chappell and believes he was responsible for his initial selection for the state.

'In 1972–73 I was in the army. I got a score against Glenelg on a difficult deck in a game that he [Chappell] was playing in. I wasn't even in the [South Australia] squad but went into the team which was a shock. The selectors didn't really want me because when I went to meet them it was, "Go to Rowe and Jarman [sports store] and get your gear – you are playing against Queensland. [But] you are 12th [man]." It wasn't a great feeling.'

The feeling Curtin had playing cricket with Chappell was that it was like a football match. He understood that approach – it was us and them. Curtin loved being out there among it especially when the crowd was booing and the opposition players hissing.

Curtin remembers well things said to him when he batted. In his first innings against Queensland, opposition captain Sam Trimble humiliated him by mockingly trying to read his name on the scoreboard and asking the others if anyone had heard of him.

'No,' came the collective response.

'You sure you are at the right ground, son?'

Similar stories are legion. Barry Jarman, when wicketkeeping for South Australia, would start a critique of a player's style.

'Geez, are you okay with your grip like that?'

It would then grow. 'Hey Rowdy, look at this bloke's grip – seems awkward to me.'

'I don't think it is his hands, Jar, it is feet that trouble me.'

David Hookes was always reminded early about his age. Would he have to finish early to go back to school? Was that his mum in the stands here to pick him up – don't want to keep her waiting.

Silence was also a tactic. A batsman who was chatty in the rooms after a day's play was frozen out when he came to the crease. He may even nod at a few drinking partners from the night before and say hello only to see them turn their backs.

Some bowlers loved the theatre. Prior hated being hit to the boundary and would curse the batsman jogging past. Thomson swore constantly but it was directed at himself for not being able to dismiss the clown with a bat. Lillee would have face-to-face moments that resulted in a droplet of perspiration falling onto the batsman's nose.

Like part of their batting technique, most players had dealt with sledging long before reaching first-class cricket. Clubs were a hotbed of chatter. When Rick Drewer was picked for Sturt he had to wear his school cap because the club had a bizarre custom that players were only awarded their club cap after their third game. He found as he took guard that the fielders were at it already. As he faced up to Glenelg's Kevin McCarthy, who opened the bowling for South Australia, he heard: 'Knock the fucking schoolboy's cap off, Macca.'

'I thought, this is a bit different,' he recalls, laughing loudly. He adapted to the sledging and came to believe an opening bowler wasn't worth his salt unless he told a batsman that he was going to knock his block off.

The commentary was designed to lever open the batsman's mind and pour some salt in – to irritate, unsettle or even amuse him. Anything to break his concentration. Was it abusive? Sometimes the wit evaporated in the scorching heat and all that was left was base-level venting. Jenner and Mallett were considered the biggest talkers in the South Australian team. Not their captain. Chappell would make comments in the field but no-one recalls there ever being an abusive attack on an opposition player.

'People get staggered and think I am away with the fairies when I say that but I never heard him speak to a player at all,' said Hookes.

This is one of the reasons why the Chappells are annoyed at references that sledging started during their years in charge. Their colourful style, ferocious play and temper of the times set them up for the label. On the eve of the 1975–76 Test series against the West Indies, Greg Chappell warned his players, through the press, to be careful of their language and behaviour.

'We have got to show restraint,' he said. 'We have reputations we don't deserve, because incidents have been blown up out of all proportions and wrongly construed.'

Chappell believes on-field comments fit into two categories; gamesmanship and abuse.

'There is a place for gamesmanship. As far as I am concerned it is intelligent use of wit, or whatever you use, to try to take advantage of a perceived weakness in an opponent. I always saw a weakness in character in an opponent as the same as a weakness outside off-stump, or a weakness against a short-pitched delivery. It is there to be exploited.

'Abuse is just mindless rubbish. There is no place for that. If it occurs the umpire should speak to the player or the captain and say, "There is a problem and if you keep it up you will be on the sheet and suspended."'

The stereotypical sledging has the batsman on the receiving end but what isn't often noted is the sledging batsmen gave bowlers. It was a different kind of mind game, of which Chappell was a master and Curtin his adoring apprentice.

'"Bounce me, dickhead." That is what he would shout as the bowler was running in,' explained Curtin.

'They couldn't help themselves and sure enough they would bounce him and he would hook them out of Sydney.'

Hookes remembered being staggered the first time he experienced it from the non-striker's end.

'He was able to abuse bowlers as they ran in – people like Hurst and Walker. He would yell out to them to bowl out-swingers or half-volleys or bouncers or whatever he wanted them to bowl.'

Cosier heard Chappell yell to him, 'You are not getting down here, it is too easy' or 'You better hop in for your chop here before they take this bloke off'.

On one occasion at the Gabba, Chappell was facing leg-spinner Malcolm Francke. The Queenslander was bowling ball after ball low and flat and Chappell met the deliveries with a dead bat. After a while Chappell shouted, 'Why don't you toss one up? I can stand here doing this all day but if you toss one up I might have a go at it.'

Francke grumbled a profanity and continued his flat deliveries and Chappell kept flat-batting them. An over after the comment, Francke lofted a delivery. Chappell skipped down the wicket and hit it back over the sightscreen for six.

'See,' he exclaimed, catching the bowler's eye, 'that could have gone anywhere.'

Another tactic was upsetting a bowler's rhythm by leaning over to brush imaginary specs of dust off the pitch while the bowler stood fuming at the top of his run.

Martin had taught his sons to find the runs in the field and so batting with Chappell was an intense and thrilling experience. For Curtin it was the greatest joy of his cricket career and his greatest education in the game.

'Once at the Adelaide Oval, he hit one past point toward the Vic Richardson Gates and off we go. He wants two. I am going to the danger end and I had a look and said "no, no, no" and sent him back. He said, "Run, you Port Adelaide shit." I said, "I am not riding a Suzuki here, mate. I am not going to make it." At the end of the over he came and said, "Let me give you a piece of advice – if in doubt run them out. I don't care if it is the Australian captain at the other end or who it is, if there is any doubt then run them out because at this level they will run you out."'

In 1975–76 Barry Curtin's chances of playing first-class cricket were fast fading. He hadn't been in the selectors' plans the entire 1974–75 season when South Australia won only one match, and now the side was flying there were no spots opening up. He batted in the middle order, and with Hookes the acknowledged wonder boy at five, and Darling taking Trevor Chappell's spot at six, the future was theirs. His chances of playing for South Australia seemed even more remote when he fractured his relationship at Port Adelaide.

After arriving at training one night in less than showroom condition he was told to leave the nets. He argued with some and then retreated to the bar where things deteriorated further. When he awoke the next morning he carried a heaving hangover and the news he would be playing for the club's B-grade on the weekend.

'I was in everyone's dog house.'

But Curtin didn't play for the Magpies' second XI. Later that day the state selectors asked him to report to the Adelaide Oval for the three-day game against the West Indies, South Australia's second match of the summer against the tourists. Chappell was having the match off and Curtin would be batting number four.

The tourists staggered through the opening day after winning the toss. Only Baichan (72), opening the innings in place of Fredericks (54) who moved down the order to number seven, made any headway in a first innings total of 188 in 42 overs.

Prior again destroyed the West Indians, claiming 6/41 including the scalps of Greenidge, Richards, Boyce and Fredericks. They were his best figures to date in first-class cricket. South Australia was 1/85 at stumps, with Drewer (50) and Cosier (7) unbeaten. As the pair returned to the middle the next morning, Curtin set up camp in the dressing room and said to anyone listening: 'You know, all I have to do is score 250 today and take six wickets tomorrow and I might be in the side to go to Perth in a few weeks.'

He was in the side in place of the form batsman in Australia, so he might as well laugh about it. Drewer added 14 before being caught behind, bringing Curtin to the crease. The West Indians were about to get a taste of Port Adelaide.

It took two-and-a-half hours, and the century was his second highest score in first-class cricket. Along the way he challenged Cosier into scoring another century against the West Indies.

'I had a bet with Cosier. He was in his thirties and we met mid-pitch. I didn't like talking when I batted because I have enough problems of my own without hearing about yours, but I called him down the track and said, "I bet you $50 if we get to 50 then I will [score a century] before you do." I knew he was a punter so his ears pricked up. At lunch I was 60, I think, and he was 48, and I said "double or nothing if we get to 100" and we both did.'

Their 156-run partnership pushed South Australia well ahead of the West Indies. Curtin enjoyed facing fast bowling and his century included nine fours and one six. As he raised his bat to acknowledge the applause, he saw Andy Roberts stretching in anticipation of the new ball. He wasn't sure he could go through it all again and when a delivery from tall off-spinner Albert Padmore was caught by Rowe he left Cosier to it.

'Cosier gets into me because I got out the last over before the second new ball and he was on 87. I was up in the box and here they come at him again. He was spewing.'

Cosier finished on 107 – his innings had been far more conservative, taking an extra 130 balls to reach effectively the same score as Curtin. Hookes added 44 and Jenner an unbeaten 50 as Woodcock declared at 8/419 at stumps.

The third and final day was batting practice for the West Indies. On Christmas Eve the tourists flew to Melbourne to prepare for the third Test. The gift for Cosier was being told he was in Australia's side and would make his Test debut in his home state. Curtin went home to celebrate Christmas at Port Adelaide and although no-one had told him, he was in the travelling party for the next Shield game against Western Australia in Perth – where, like him, the game is played loud.

CHAPTER SEVEN

CHANGING ALLEGIANCES

Western Australia v. South Australia, Perth, January 16–19, 1976

When Gary Cosier walked into Australia's dressing room at the MCG on Boxing Day 1975 the first person to say hello was Jeff Thomson. The friendly demeanour masked an agony in Thommo's personal life. During the Perth Test he had received news his flatmate from Brisbane had died while playing in a Brisbane grade match for Toombul. Martin Bedkober was hit in the chest by a ball and suffered a fatal heart attack at the wicket. It was declared a 'freak accident' by specialists. The toll of this dangerous sport was now real and personal. The funeral had been held in the week before the Melbourne Test. The man who said he liked seeing blood on the pitch didn't seem so cavalier anymore.

Outside the rooms almost 85,000 people were filling the ground. They were in party mode and beer flowed as freely as larrikin antics. There were several streakers, including one who offered his tinny to umpire Jack Collins at square leg. The sound of a steel-drum band wafted through the outer. By the final session authorities struggled to control outbreaks of behaviour associated more with the winter game.

The Chappell brothers were the only Australians to have scored Test centuries against the travelling West Indies and Greg didn't fancy batting on a green MCG deck. When he won the toss he went against his grandfather's instructions and put the West Indies in. Rod Marsh began taping his hands, including putting pieces of polystyrene around his fingers. He had said to Thommo: 'It hurts but I love it.' After the day's play he would lay steaks over his hands to ease the swelling and bruising.

Despite his fearsome reputation, Thommo was far from the best bowler so far in the series. He had taken four wickets, the same as Michael Holding, but Dennis Lillee had eight and Andy Roberts 12. Before the first Test Thommo had a $500 bet with a West Indian businessman that he would end the series with more wickets than Roberts. In a celebration of ferocity he started making up ground on day one of the third Test. He bowled 13 no balls and a wide but dismissed five of the first six batsmen – Fredericks (59), Greenidge (3), Rowe (0), Kallicharran (20) and Lloyd (2). Lillee collected four. The West Indies survived 47 overs and made 224.

Cosier's moment came early in the final session of the second day. At 4.10pm he walked through the gates and onto the MCG as an Australian Test cricketer. The home side was 4/188. He passed

Ian Redpath who was returning after scoring 102. At stumps Cosier (44) and Greg Chappell (42) were not out.

Their partnership went to 114 and steered Australia into a commanding position. After Chappell went on the third day, Marsh continued the work. Cosier was 99 at lunch and spent an agonising 40 minutes in the rooms contemplating which way the next moment would go. It went well. In the first over after lunch he clipped a ball from Roberts past point to go over 100 and claim membership of a group of less than a dozen men who had scored centuries on debut. When he was out, caught Kallicharran, bowled Roberts for 109, Australia was 6/390. Thommo added 44 at the end to set a total of 485.

Despite a century from Lloyd the West Indies couldn't match it. Australia won by eight wickets. Less than a week later in Sydney, Australia won the fourth Test by seven wickets. Greg Chappell made 182 in the first innings. Thommo ripped the opposition apart in the second innings taking 6/50 with only three West Indian batsmen managing to get into double figures.

*

After Australia clinched the series against the West Indies attention returned to the Sheffield Shield. Queensland was still the favourite to take the competition as it was sitting atop the table with 69 points ahead of South Australia (54), Western Australia (43), New South Wales (38) and Victoria (35).

But Greg Chappell's side had already played five matches,

while Victoria had played four, and New South Wales five – which suggested the latter two states were out of the running. However, South Australia and Western Australia had played only three games each, and now the two states were scheduled to play back-to-back matches that could decide if either was able to challenge Queensland for the Shield title. As South Australia flew to Perth for the first match up, Victoria was frustrating the home side in Brisbane. In a rain-affected draw Queensland could only gather seven bonus points while Victoria collected six.

Travelling west was not something Ashley Mallett enjoyed. Not because he disliked returning to his childhood state but because he suffered anxiety attacks when flying. Team mates got used to Mallett shutting everyone's window on the plane before takeoff so he didn't have to see the ground fall away beneath him. He endured flying as a white-knuckle necessity.

Similar episodes of shortness of breath and palpitating heart would arrive without warning when he was fielding. There was no clue as to why they came on or when they would disappear. Only when he was in the action, it seemed, did things clear up. Mallett endured his anxiety attacks in silence for fear that admitting to them may jeopardise his place in the side.

Mallett was a popular teammate whose dry asides earned him the nickname 'Rowdy'. Bespectacled, tall and wiry, he looked more like an academic than a sportsman. He loved writing and, to fulfil an ambition to make a career out of it, he began working for a suburban newspaper in 1975.

To add to his unlikely demeanour as a cricketer, Mallett had a reputation for being uncoordinated and his clumsy episodes were collected and joyfully recounted by team mates. One of his most notorious moments came in a critical match against New South Wales in 1971. The visitors were 1/86 chasing 320 on the last day. Chappell's intention was to bowl Mallett most of the day on a deteriorating wicket. However, there was a problem. While fielding a ball Mallett managed to step on his own right hand and put his spikes through his spinning fingers.

Mallett's ironic manner deflected a deep knowledge of the sport, one in which his success was hard earned. While many players followed a linear path to success, Mallett had to make bold decisions. He watched Terry Jenner play for Western Australia, while he could only manage two matches carrying the drinks. Who was the best spinner in Australia? Clarrie Grimmett. Maybe he could help, Mallett figured.

So he caught the train across the Nullarbor and tracked down the old wizard. Grimmett was an eccentric character who once nutted out the timing of every traffic signal between the Adelaide Oval and his house and calibrated his driving speed so that he never encountered a red light on the drive home.

Grimmett was 76 when Mallett turned up at his place. The leggie had a pitch in the backyard but was up a tree hanging a ball on a rope when the visitor arrived. He clambered down and was all business.

'We got to the nets and he had an old Jack Hobbs bat, no gloves, no protector or pads, and [he was] wearing his horn-rimmed glasses,' recalls Mallett.

'"Righto son," he cried. So I bowled and he played forward and it hit the middle of the bat. He said "Come here" and I walked down the pitch expecting some insight. He said, "Give up bowling and become a batsman." I said, "Hang on, I've only bowled one ball," and he said "Oh I can tell you've got no variety."'

To prove his point Grimmett tied a handkerchief over his eyes and successfully played the next ball blindfolded. The old coot was right – and wrong. Mallett needed to work on variations and, together in Grimmett's backyard, they did so. The key to it was lifting the ball above the batman's eyes so he couldn't easily pick up the landing place. Within a year Mallett was in the Australian XI and for the next decade was the finest slow bowler in the country.

Dennis Yagmich loved keeping to Mallett because he says he bowled to the gloves, nestled next to the off-stump.

'He used a lot of guile, threw the ball up and he bowled to the keeper a lot. Guys don't do that now, they dart it in. But if you threw it up the keeper gets justice. Ashley wasn't a big turner but the away ball, the drifter that got nicks and stumpings, was beautiful.'

From his position Yagmich appreciated the craft of the tandem spinners and the different personalities involved. TJ would tell Chappell that you could tell which one had the advantage of bowling into the wind by their hair, pointing out that Mallett was receding from the front and he had a bald patch developing at the back.

'There was always friction between TJ and Ian because Ian favoured Ashley and gave him first chance with the ball. TJ would get upset from time to time. Listening to TJ and Rowdy on the field was fun but quite embarrassing at times. It was a privilege to keep to both these guys.'

He also recalls the embarrassment he felt sitting in the rooms listening to Jenner at the start of the season. TJ was in an ebullient mood and he stood up on the training table to say a few words. He looked around the room and said, 'Just before we go out I would like to welcome the South Australians to the side'.

Yagmich was sitting between Chappell and Woodcock. The tension he felt about the wisecrack eased when he heard his captain chuckling.

Like Jenner and Mallett, Yagmich left Western Australian in search of opportunity. He was a good keeper but was stuck behind the best in the country. In 1972–73 Yagmich played three games for Western Australia when Rod Marsh was in the West Indies. At the end of the season state selector Hugh Bevan apologised for dropping him but explained, 'When Rod is back we can't play you anymore.'

Unlike Queensland, which had begun its futile pursuit of the Shield in 1926–27, Western Australia had immediate success in first-class cricket, winning the competition in its first season (1947–48). After that, though, the state struggled for respect and identity. Few players were given a chance at international level and the WACA was lumped with the cost of paying the transport costs of bringing states from the east to play in Perth. Things began changing in the 1960s when Graham McKenzie became Australia's first-ball bowler. Perth's first Test match was played in 1970 and within a few years there were more Western Australian representatives in the Test XI than any other state.

The side Yagmich played for won the Shield that season, one of five times it did so during the 1970s. Perth grade cricket was renowned for the truest wickets in the country and along with dry conditions it meant the quality (and quantity) of play was high.

Exporting players surplus to requirements wasn't a problem. When Jenner asked his former captain Barry Shepherd if he was being disloyal by leaving the west, Shepherd replied that the loyalty should be to himself, adding that when he retired the WACA gave him an electric kettle in thanks for 11 years of service.

It was similar advice Yagmich heard from his father: 'You need to do what is best for you.' His old man always seemed to make the right decisions. The Yagmich family had come to Western Australia from Croatia in the early 20th century and brought with them a tradition of winemaking going back hundreds of years on the Dalmatian Coast. Jakov Yagmich arrived in Kalgoorlie in 1922 and worked towards the passage for his wife and son to join him. It took eight years for him to save enough to see them again. Ned Yagmich was 12 years old when he was reunited with his father in 1934. He wanted to follow his heritage in the new country and in 1947 bought a property in the Swan Valley to grow wine grapes and raise his family.

The area was perfect for kids who liked being outdoors. Dennis Yagmich's childhood friend was Tony Mann whose father was a winemaker next door at Houghton's winery. Together they played cricket and made their way through the grades until Mann was selected in the Western Australian side and, in doing so, took the leg-spinning place coveted by Jenner.

When Ned Yagmich suggested that his son leave the state he proposed New South Wales or South Australia. Word spread and, with Mike Hendricks likely ending his playing time in South Australia, it seemed the latter state was his best option. He was given no promises but he joined Bradman's old club Kensington because they also needed a gloveman.

Yagmich was an accountant and soon found work. He also tallied up hours and hours in the nets to improve his fielding and batting. He was picked for the game at the Adelaide Oval against Victoria in February 1975 and took eight catches in a losing side. The job was now his.

Unlike Marsh, who was verbose behind the stumps, Yagmich was gentle and quietly spoken. He was a deep thinker and recognised Chappell as a rough diamond who didn't suffer fools and who was straight down the line. If you needed help then he sat down and helped you. From his perch behind the stumps he saw Chappell lay out a day's play with craft and cunning.

'Ian was a brilliant captain. I played under Tony Lock and Keith Slater but, to me, Ian was the great captain. He led by example, he was a man's man and was very astute. He was spot on with field placings and he really knew the opposition; he knew what everybody did.'

Although he was one for action not words, for some reason Chappell predicted a good result for the trip to Perth, telling Jenner he would get 150. When he won the toss and batted, Chappell returned to the WACA rooms, padded up and lay down for a massage. It never really got started. Although Lillee was returning from a bout of pleurisy that had kept him out of the Sydney Test match, he was lively enough to have Drewer caught at gully on the fourth ball of the day. In a repeat of the second Test match, the South Australian captain was in early. Aside from Lillee, the home side boasted paceman Wayne Clark, seamers Terry Alderman and Ian Brayshaw, and leggie Bob Paulsen. Chappell flayed them all.

After a 90-run partnership with Woodcock he teamed with Cosier to quicken the pace. The two men were in-form and although he was older it was Chappell who ran hardest, pushing the score past 200. Their partnership of 124 came in 93 minutes. When Cosier departed on 94 in came Hookes, who lashed out to make 44 before being caught brilliantly by Kim Hughes at mid-off.

Chappell's 117 (off 173 balls) included 20 fours and a six. When he reached three figures he passed his grandfather's tally of 18 centuries scored for South Australia. Late in the day he mistimed a hook off Alderman that floated to Paulsen at square leg.

As he arrived back in the rooms he was confronted by Jenner.

'You lied to me.'

'What are you talking about?'

'You said 150, not 117.'

At the 65-over mark, and with 20 minutes remaining in the day, South Australia was 4/308 having earned six batting points while Western Australia had two bowling points. Chappell didn't declare. He thought the pitch was playing perfectly and the time would have only allowed his bowlers about four overs. He declared at stumps at 7/330.

As the players drank and smoked, the umpires Don Hawks and Gary Duperouzel were asked by reporters if they were going to report Chappell for an incident during the day. When he had reached 99, Chappell had repeated his performance from the first match against New South Wales, dropping his strides to make adjustments. The publicity from the first episode had reverberated for some time. A cartoon by Paul Rigby of News Limited, syndicated around Australia, had the Australian side all in fielding positions with their pants around their ankles. The curious West Indian batsmen are looking around saying, 'It's either support for Chappelli or some sort of political comment.'

The umpires declined a report, explaining that they felt 'it was a legitimate thing that Chappell did'.

Lillee only bowled 15 overs in the innings, at less than express pace, to return 1/91. Phil Ridings had accompanied the South Australian team in his capacity as a national selector and he sat in the grandstand watching Lillee to see if he would be fit for the fifth Test match which started the following Friday in Adelaide.

The question over Lillee's fitness also asked if Wayne Prior would be ready as his replacement if needed. Prior versus the

Western Australian batsmen was a perfect audition. He was fast and this was the WACA, so he let it all hang out, and split Western Australia's vaunted batting asunder.

Bruce Laird was caught behind for six, Hughes nicked one to Chappell at first slip for one, Robbie Langer mistimed a hook that went into the bowler's hands for a duck, Brayshaw was caught by Jenner at point for 13, then Lillee went the same way for nought. In between, Cosier bowled Wally Edwards after a solid 52 and Ric Charlesworth was run out for five.

In the first hour after lunch Marsh and Clark stood in the middle with the score at 8/97. Fang steamed in again but strayed down leg. Marsh glanced the ball to help it on its way to the boundary to bring three figures to the total. When he looked back up the wicket, he saw Prior on the ground, slowly getting to his feet and moving gingerly. He had lost his footing in the follow through and his ankle twisted under the force. Several deliveries earlier he had thrown his boot out to stop a drive and caught its full force on his ankle. He finished the over and tried to bowl another but the jagged pain was too much. He limped off the ground with 5/44 off 11.1 overs.

Chappell put them straight back in after Western Australia was all out for 161. A ninth innings stand between Marsh and Clark of 39 after Prior's exit made things respectable. Without their spearhead, though, South Australia couldn't break through, and at stumps Western Australia was 1/89.

The following morning a doctor put several long syringes into Fang's ankle to numb the pain.

'So I went out and got about three overs out of the jab and got a wicket but it wore off. You had to be on the ground for a certain time so I went to first slip and when it was time to bowl I came off and got another jab and took another wicket. I did that three times. Then the Western Australian doctor said, "Nah, I can't give you any more because I've done it three times." Three pain killers and three wickets. He must have thought, "Nah, don't give them any more."'

Marsh hated losing to anyone, especially Chappell, and his batsmen showed application and doggedness in building a total. The top five all got solid starts and when Marsh batted he did so flamboyantly. He calculated setting South Australia a final day target of between 200 and 250 which, given his attack, could be enough.

In his last over before tea, Prior bounced Marsh and the Western Australia skipper couldn't resist. His hook shot sailed to Attenborough at fine leg. The players adjourned to the rooms (Western Australia 5/249) for the break before returning for the final session.

It took only 35 minutes: Lillee 0, Clark 8, Langer 64, Paulsen 0, Brayshaw 5. Western Australia was all out for 268 and had a lead of 100 runs. Attenborough took 4/61 in his best figures for South Australia, and Prior had 3/24 off nine overs with three maidens. Wounded ankle and all, he had written his name as starkly as he could in Phil Riding's notebook.

Whether Lillee felt he needed to prove anything is unknown but he came out at full throttle. With the 'Doctor' howling at his back his pace was vicious. In his first over a delivery hit a crack and whipped off Woodcock's leading elbow. The opener immediately lost all feeling in his forearm and was forced from the field. The damage was more than fleeting. In the months to follow his arm grew weaker to the point where he didn't have the strength to even turn a key in a door or pick up his briefcase.

In Lillee's second over he reared one up at Rick Drewer. The opener thought it was going to kill him, and so swayed back to avoid the ball and, in doing so, took his bottom hand off his bat. The ball hit his glove and flew to Langer at second slip. He led a chorus of appeals. In the millisecond of the moment the umpire could only see a deflection and so gave Drewer out.

Drewer was steamed-up when leaving the field; in part because he wasn't technically out, as he wasn't holding the bat, but also because he had completed a pair. When he got into the change rooms he threw his bat down and cursed the 'cheating' Western Australian umpires. Mallett looked at him and said, 'Don't worry, Stumpy, you are a bloody lot safer in here than you are out there.' The quip made him laugh and he sat down to watch the next victim go to the crease. It was Rick Darling.

Chappell had promoted the teenager so as not to upset the batting list too much late in the day. With the reincarnation of 'The Demon' Fred Spofforth charging full steam downwind, Chappell had one opener injured and the other out for a blob with only one run on the board.

This is why he was astonished when Darling stepped inside the line of a short ball from Lillee and hooked it to the boundary for four. In the rooms the South Australians watched open-mouthed. Chappell, at the non-striker's end, had his mouth open too.

'Doesn't look too good mate, does it?' he started. 'The best fast bowler in the world getting hooked by an 18-year-old.'

Lillee glared at Chappell and returned to his mark. His next ball was short and fast. Darling played an even better shot that went like a bullet to the square-leg fence.

'Oh it is looking real bad now, mate. The best fast bowler in the world is being hooked by an 18-year old,' he repeated teasingly.

The glare grew more intense. Chappell knew that the difference between Lillee and other fast bowlers was that while he would get angry he would keep thinking. The next ball was a beautiful outswinger that beat Darling cold. Lillee swung around mid-pitch and looked straight at Chappell and said: 'Two out of three ain't bad,' and they shared a laugh.

Darling made it to stumps, but the next day Alderman had him caught for 29. Chappell was unbeaten on 67. He scored the winning runs by emphatically driving Alderman for four with two full sessions still available. His side had now beaten every state outright, and the past two on their home decks. The wins against the other states were epic contests fought on razor edges but this was different; this was a destruction of the best side in the country.

South Australia was playing cricket the way their captain ordained it – fierce, smart and gutsy. He showed them the wall and they ran at it. South Australia, the easy beats of recent seasons, had walked into the fast-forward world of the WACA and taken 21 points to Western Australia's two. It effectively killed off any chance of Western Australia taking a hat-trick of Shield titles, and with a tropical downpour almost certainly robbing Queensland of ten points against Victoria, only one point separated Queensland and South Australia, and the Chappell brothers, atop the Sheffield Shield table.

CHAPTER EIGHT

MONEY MATTERS

South Australia v. Western Australia,
Adelaide, February 14–17, 1976

The Chappell brothers weren't great ones for pre-match oration. Gary Cosier says a big speech from Ian was, 'You blokes ready?'

Fortunately for them there was a man who took on that role in the Adelaide rooms. When he stood up to make the speech before the fifth Test against the West Indies the Australians listened with respect, even though the man talking had never played cricket anywhere but the beach or the backyard.

Barry Rees grew up in a time when there were jobs found for young men who couldn't easily navigate school or society. His great love was sport, the one subject in which he could remember things and converse with others, but not an easy area for his father, Ray Rees, to find him somewhere to work. In 1960 David

Rowe and South Australian wicketkeeper Barry Jarman opened a sports store in the city. Ray Rees knew the pair and one day asked them whether there might be any work at their store that Barry could manage. The partners thought that maybe he could sweep the floors, get the lunches and run errands. Jarman asked the teenager who his favourite sportsman was. He replied that it was Keith Miller.

'Nugget Miller,' he said. 'Then we will call you Nugget.'

Rees was a happy, likeable teenager and would do anything they asked. When Ray came to collect his son after work he was shocked to hear that Barry had been running messages during the day. In a mild panic he explained that his son didn't understand traffic lights and it was too dangerous.

'Well he has been doing it for three weeks,' said Jarman.

When Jarman took him to the Adelaide Oval a world opened up that no-one from either side could have anticipated. Nugget was allowed into the rooms and sat side by side with the best cricketers in the country, ones who accepted him and enjoyed his company. They handed him gear and he sat wearing pads, gloves and a baggy green cap given to him by Norm O'Neill.

Jarman further expanded Nugget's world by inviting him on an away trip with South Australia. Ray Rees paid for the travel but Jarman put him up in his room and covered his costs. All of a sudden the boy who had no reason to be in the rooms was a permanent presence.

Somewhere along the way curiosity and sympathy matured into trust and love. When he first came into the dressing rooms

Rick Darling was shy about his place and held back. Nugget helped him adjust and Darling calls him a 'loyal friend'.

Although he would happily run errands, fetch cold drinks or bags of ice, Nugget's role wasn't that of a lackey. Jarman, Favell and Chappell didn't treat him that way and so neither did the players. John Inverarity saw the significance during his time in South Australia after starting his career in Western Australia.

'When a young man breaks into first-class cricket, and whether he's playing for South Australia or Victoria or Western Australia, part of that is then becoming a part of what is this cocoon in which Nugget resides. Part of the rite of passage is to become associated with Nugget and with that comes the responsibility ... of looking after Nugget.

'They have a sense of how Nugget is different and they just treasure his presence. There is that team dynamic. There is that chemistry and when Nugget is present he enhances that chemistry in some way. When he is present a lot of bonding takes place. He facilitates good relationships between people. He facilitates a bond at a higher level.'

Geoff Attenborough remembers him easing tensions and never having a bad word about others.

'He knew when to shut up, too. The boys looked after him – a couple of times there was almost a punch-up over Nug because someone said something about him within ear shot and the boys didn't take kindly to that.'

By 1975 Nugget had assumed the role of pre-session orator. Chappell would tell him to get up on the table and 'rev the boys up'. In a halting, repetitive speech he would remind the players that dropped catches lose matches, to keep their eye on the captain and do what he says, to keep the throws up to the keeper, to get there and make runs, for the bowlers to back up fielders, and to get plenty of runs. It ended with applause and sometimes the players would, as a lark, pull the chairs away from the table to leave him marooned.

After winning the toss, electing to bat and listening to Nugget, the Australians won the fifth Test match by 190 runs. Redpath (103) and Gilmour (95) set up a first innings total of 418. Thommo took four wickets as the Windies were out for 274. Alan Turner played the finest innings of his Test career making 136 in the second dig, and the total of 7/345 put the game beyond the crumbling tourists. The only sign of life was Viv Richards moving up to open with Fredericks and scoring 101.

There was a hiccup for South Australia, however. After making 37 on the first day of the fifth Test, Cosier bowled five overs on the second. That night his back ached and it was still sore after the third day, a day he spent in the dressing room as Greg Chappell had re-jigged the order to keep him inside. On the rest day doctors confirmed he had a displaced vertebra. His summer of joy was turning sour. In a one-day game against Queensland earlier in the month he had tripped over the boundary rope chasing a ball and went full force into the fence, damaging his neck and leaving him with severe headaches.

The back injury cost him a place in the Australian side for the final Test in Melbourne, and he was replaced by Rick McCosker. In that match, another hundred from Redpath set up an opening

351. The West Indies were now running on fumes and managed only 160 in reply. Lillee finished with eight wickets for the match as the Australians won by 165 runs. Thomson collected his $500, finishing the series with 29 wickets ahead of Lillee with 27 and Roberts with 22.

In the final inning, Greg Chappell stood in the centre of the MCG unbeaten on 54. His first summer in charge of Australia had been brilliant. Having arrived on the back of their World Cup win as the biggest threat to Australia's claim as the world's best side, the West Indies had been dismantled 5–1. Greg Chappell had scored 702 runs at an average of 117 while the next best batsmen were Ian Redpath with 575 at 52 and Ian Chappell with 449 at 45. For Chappell, the only remaining accomplishment needed to end this perfect season would be to deliver Queensland its first Sheffield Shield.

*

The Chappell brothers did more than play cricket while in Melbourne in the first week of February 1976. On the rest day of the fifth Test they went to the Hilton Hotel overlooking the MCG where they met their former Australian teammate Bob Cowper.

Cowper's nickname was 'Wallaby' because of his family's involvement with rugby union. His father, Denis, had captained the national side in South Africa in 1933. The amateur tradition of the sport seeped into Cowper's thinking about cricket and he believed in the ideals of playing for love, not money. However, this masked a deep understanding of commerce and economics. He thought widely about the game and its finances and found Ian Chappell an interested listener.

Although he wasn't captain in the 1960s, Chappell played a pivotal role in a rare inflammatory push for better conditions for Test players. In 1969 Australia toured India winning 3–1. It took its toll though and the players were in poor nick when they continued on to South Africa for a four-Test series against the best side in the world.

The Australian players were so worn out from travel and illness that Captain Bill Lawry watched in agony as his exhausted bowler Graham McKenzie was unable to get the ball past the edge of a bat. The Springboks belted the Australians and were enjoying things so much they asked for a fifth Test to be arranged. The Australian Cricket Board was happy to oblige but the team, in particular Chappell, resisted.

The players had already voiced their concerns through a letter from Lawry to the board about the poor touring conditions in India. Chappell saw the proposed fifth Test as a rare chance to stand up, because the contracts they had signed only paid them for four Test matches in South Africa. As he saw it, a fifth game would have to be negotiated.

The ACB offered $200 per player in payment – the players wanted $500. The board stood firm but the Wanderers Club in Johannesburg offered subsidies to push the payment to $500 in an obvious sign of the Australians' value. Chappell exhorted the team to resist the lure – to stand up for their rights or risk being pushed around for the rest of their careers. At one stage he pulled out his own cheque book and offered to make up the difference to each of them to make a point. Lawry said he needed a unanimous decision to play and so without it he refused to agree to the extra match. Not much had progressed in the six years since.

In that time though, Australia was going through its highest period of inflation since the war. For a decade from 1968, the cost of living rose by about 9 per cent per year, peaking in the second half of 1975 at 18 per cent.

During the 1974–75 Ashes series Chappell became so enraged that, while monster crowds were turning up to Test matches, his strike bowler Dennis Lillee was struggling to make ends meet because of all the time he had to put into cricket. The board added a bonus $200 per Test match for each player. Lillee believed that the Test players deserved $30,000 as a minimum salary.

Economics had played a part in Bob Cowper retiring. In 1968, when he was 27, he stood down from Test cricket. He was working as a merchant banker and stockbroker and there wasn't enough reward from full-time cricket. He captained Victoria to the Shield title in 1969–70 and then walked away from the game. It was a rational rather than emotional decision. He figured out that in 1968 he had played cricket for Australia for nine months of the year and earned $3,000. That was unsustainable.

By 1975, when the Australian players were still scratching around for pin money, Cowper was a highly-successful businessman who wasn't meeting the Chappells to talk about line and length. The Chappells wanted to formalise their agitation and sought Cowper's counsel. They were joined by Rod Marsh, Rick McCosker and Bob Hawke, who was president of the Australian Council of Trade Unions. Hawke understood that the situation was textbook 'labour versus capital' – a fight for wages and conditions. With the Labor Party having just been trounced at the polls, and Gough Whitlam's ratings at a low ebb, Hawke counselled against setting up a players' union for fear of backlash. Instead he proposed establishing a players' association to advocate as a collective with one person to liaise between the parties.

Given his business nous, Cowper agreed to conduct negotiations on matters such as payments, promotion, sponsorships and tour schedules. Paperwork was drawn up that would be put to each player asking them to appoint Cowper as their representative.

In the twilight of his career as a player, time was running out for Chappell to look after his boys. Prior to the 1972 Ashes tour Ray Steele had reminded him that whatever happened that winter, history would remember it as Ian Chappell's Australians, not the 1972 Australians. It made him aware that while the game was long in its history, his time to influence it was short. The off-field decisions that affected players had to be worn on the field by the captain.

One of the spats that had floored him was in 1974 when New Zealand toured and the Australian selectors replaced Ian Redpath with Ian Davis at number six. Later they restored Redpath but wanted him to open. Chappell felt humiliated as a captain and uncomfortable talking to a loyal teammate about the changes.

'I had to go and ask him to open the batting. It was so embarrassing [but] he was great. Redders could have told me to get stuffed after being dropped at six but he didn't, he agreed to open. He had been treated just like a number in the team. That is why I got annoyed. Who was the muggins who had to try to hold the whole thing together and keep the team spirit together as captain while they [board and selectors] are doing all this crap to you? So that is why I didn't have a lot of respect for administration. To me you were just treated as a number.'

The question of payments rumbled along as Western Australia arrived in Adelaide for the return match against South Australia. Coincidentally, on the day the Federal Arbitration Commission awarded workers a 6.4 per cent pay rise, the Australian Cricket Board confirmed it was opening the vault and paying $400 bonus for those who had played in all six Test matches against the West Indies. Alan Barnes used the announcement to explain that senior or long-term players who played all matches would get more than $8,000 from Australian and state boards.

When asked about the $8,000 he would receive, Marsh said it was 'a good beginning but I would like to see $28,000'.

'I doubt very much whether the Australian Cricket Board could fail to hand out a far greater remuneration to the players if there was a repeat series against the West Indies and we attracted the same crowds.'

Gary Cosier didn't qualify for the bonus. Despite his crook back he went to Melbourne for the final Test where he saw a specialist. The prognosis was that he might be able to bat but that he shouldn't be asked to bowl. After three days at the MCG he flew to Adelaide for a second opinion. This specialist suggested the trouble was with his hips and that they were creating strain upstream in one of his vertebrae. After some manipulation he felt sweet relief. His only real concern was quick bending and so suggested to Chappell he might be tucked away in a quieter spot in the field.

The injuries to Cosier and Prior had Chappell worried. In the nets he told Hookes to mark out a longer run, figuring he may need from him a few overs of medium pace at some stage.

Chappell won the toss and batted. After the brilliant win in Perth a victory at home would both knock the Western Australians out of Shield contention and give South Australia a rails run to the finish. That is what it would have done if Lillee wasn't bowling. On a pitch that had more grass on it, and produced more bounce, than the Test wicket a fortnight earlier, Lillee was unplayable.

His 7/41 off less than ten overs had the job done just before 2.30pm. South Australia was all out for 87 – its worst ever score against Western Australia at the Adelaide Oval.

Drewer (0), Darling (2), Jenner (2) Mallett (12), Yagmich (1) and Attenborough (4) all brought joy to the quick but it was when he speared one down leg side and saw it deflect off Chappell's glove and into Marsh's gloves that it was clear whose wicket meant the most to Lillee. Marsh clicked his heels together and roosted the ball into the heavens while Lillee leapt mid-pitch with his arms raised in evangelical praise of the gods of seam.

Western Australia was 4/127 at stumps. The South Australians put the poor day behind them and claimed quick wickets on the second day. Mallett ended with 5/68 as Western Australia's innings was wound up at 177, giving it a lead of 90. The off-spinner's mix of containment and aggression was superb. His 27 overs included eight maidens and he took the wickets of four of the top six batsmen. A ninth-wicket, 26-run partnership from Lillee and Paulsen earned the visitors the only batting point awarded for the match.

A disaster for the home side awaited them in the rooms. Prior's ankle injury had flared again after just seven overs and he was out of the game. Drewer went to face his nemesis. After three ducks on end to Lillee he was desperate for runs and the side needed a strong foundation. The key for him was to first occupy the crease. Lillee was fast, accurate and smart, and every delivery asked a question that demanded the right answer. Drewer scratched around for five before feeling an outswinger touch the edge. Brayshaw's catch in the slips signalled the end. The man who had waited so long to be awarded a cap in first-class cricket was finished after two seasons.

When Chappell was caught and bowled Brayshaw for 17, it was Woodcock who took control of the innings. He batted out the day, spending almost four hours in the middle. A partnership of 79 in 101 minutes with the out-of-sorts Cosier was followed by a brisk 37-run combination with Darling. At stumps a day of revival had put South Australia 73 runs ahead with seven wickets in hand and two days to play.

Time was on the side of Woodcock as he faced Lillee on the third morning. The fast bowler jogged in and rolled his arm over with a loosener to open proceedings. Perhaps spooked by the medium pace, Woodcock played all over the ball and was clean bowled. Moments later Darling played a loose stroke outside off stump and Lillee had 2/5 and had barely got out of second gear. Jenner was promoted up the order but made only eight.

Hookes stayed for 72 balls to make 18 before being caught behind off Lillee, who had taken the new ball. South Australia's lead was 114 and its innings looked to be in a tailspin until an unlikely and belligerent cameo from Ashley Mallett stiffened things up. He stood up to the attack for almost an hour and a half, along the way growling and barking at Lillee, Marsh, and anyone else who came within range. Although they were long-time national team mates there was history at play here, and a little amateur theatrics too.

The previous season when the two states met in Perth, Lillee had bounced Mallett mercilessly. Several deliveries hit him on the gloves leaving his hands badly bruised. Mallett knew that if he had been picked for the first Test against England that he wouldn't have been able to play.

Although most saw Mallett as a gentlemanly type, Chappell knew there was some mongrel in the offie and he admired how Mallett found his own way to bite back.

'I knew Rowdy could bat but he used to get the shits when people bounced him a lot. Not because he was scared but because as an off-spinner he couldn't retaliate.

'He used to throw the bat. I had seen him do it in Test cricket. If there was a bat pad in, he would play the ball and make sure he let the bat go … in the general direction of the bat pad. That was Rowdy's way of fighting back.'

When Lillee bounced him at Adelaide, the short-forward square-leg Ric Charlesworth had to duck for cover to avoid wearing the bat. As Lillee steamed in for the next ball, Mallett backed away from the stumps to both irritate and wear down the bowler. The first part worked anyway.

'I did it to give Lillee the shits,' explained Mallett.

'I asked for the sightscreen to be moved – they said it is permanently fixed so you can't move it. I said okay, don't worry about it then. Marsh said, "If you ever do that to my fast bowler again I will instruct him to run through the crease and bowl straight at your head." So I refused to take up my stance again until Marsh stopped talking. I said to [umpire Robin] Bailhache, "Can you to tell that fat, moustachioed prick to shut up otherwise I am not facing."'

Predictably the next ball was short and fast and hit Mallett on his bowling hand. In a moment of pain and frustration Mallett pulled the glove off and threw it away. As Charlesworth went over and bent down to collect it, Marsh shouted at him, 'Don't touch it, son.'

Mallett leaned back on his bat and said, 'Doesn't worry me, we are playing for time. We could be here for weeks.'

Amid the histrionics the umpires took control, the glove was returned and play resumed. Another short one from Lillee took the bat out of Mallett's hand, but this time he was using it to defend his face.

Mallett's eventual satisfaction, when leaving the crease on 29 after being caught behind, was that it was Malone and not Lillee who had got him to snick one. South Australia was all out for 239. Lillee ended the innings with 5/72 and 12/113 for the game.

If Chappell needed any more signs of a team remade in his own image then the final innings of this hairy-chested battle provided it as they tried to defend 150 against the best state in Australia. Without Prior he handed the new ball to Cosier who, despite medical opinions that he shouldn't be bowling, took 3/9 in his first four overs, collecting Laird, Yardley and Marsh.

Mallett caught and bowled Edwards, and then collected two wickets in one over. The first was Langer (4) caught brilliantly by Attenborough at mid-on, followed by Charlesworth caught behind for a duck. Western Australia was reeling at 6/62.

Kim Hughes remained at the crease and was joined by Brayshaw. The sight of Hughes playing enthusiastically stuck in Mallett's craw a bit. The young schoolteacher had played during the 1973–74 season at East Torrens after falling out of favour in Western Australia. He had a reputation as a beautiful if impetuous batsman, and when he couldn't make the state XI he decided impulsively to switch states mid-season. Mallett was among those who heard word of the talent at East Torrens but, despite hints being dropped with selectors, Hughes was never invited to train with the South Australian squad, and at season's end he headed back to Perth.

Now he and Brayshaw put on a 90-run partnership to win the match for Western Australia. They did it in the face of two dropped catches and Chappell's attempt to go off at six o'clock when 24 runs were still needed. As the captain started leading his side off the umpires, Bailhache and Alan Crapp, told him to continue playing, and 22 minutes later everyone was shaking hands. The umpires handed in their sheets with Lillee reported for an outburst against Mallett after a not out decision, and Marsh reported for abusive language directed at a supporter.

The victory gave Western Australia 16 points, putting them third on Shield table with 62 points and back in contention. Queensland was second with 76, behind South Australia with 79. Although his side only collected four points, Chappell could live with the result because his theory was that you needed to win five games to take the Shield and if you did that the other three games didn't matter. With Victoria next up at home, followed by the testing east coast tour of Sydney and Brisbane, he had games up his sleeve. But he was running out of players. For consecutive matches Prior hadn't been able to bowl out both innings because of what had now been diagnosed as a chipped bone in his ankle. The next match started in three days and so a new player was added to the squad – a 25-year-old Victorian-raised quick named Rodney Hogg.

CHAPTER NINE

AN ENDURING KNOCK

South Australia v. Victoria, Adelaide, February 20–23, 1976

The match between South Australia and Victoria in which Rodney Hogg made his first-class debut started with rancour and ended in rebellion, and in between some heroic and exacting cricket was played.

At the end of his career Hogg would look back with a broad perspective and declare it among the greatest contests in which he had ever taken part. Barry Curtin believed it was how the game should be played and he wished 'you could just bottle it'.

The pair of mavericks had come into the side in place of Wayne Prior and Rick Drewer. In the nets, warming up, Curtin still wasn't sure if he would be carrying the drinks for the third consecutive match. As the players drifted toward the changing rooms Chappell approached him.

'Baz, you have got the job.'

Curtin was crestfallen in the belief that he was 12th man again and it showed in his body language.

'Relax. You are opening.'

That is when the panic set in. Curtin had never opened in his career. After Chappell won the toss he unusually chose to field. This suited Hogg.

'I did not like Victoria,' recalls the Victorian.

Making his first-class debut Hogg was 24, six feet tall and a bundle of prickling energy. His chest on action drew on everything he had. His humour and attitude were like his bowling. He spoke his mind and did his own thing. Gary Cosier knew him best from playing at Northcote.

'Hogg was different. Leaving Thommo out of it, he was as quick as anyone I have seen. Always his own man – he would get picked and then wouldn't go to training. He was insular as a character and a little hard to control but a great player.'

Hogg's frustration at not being picked for Victoria started getting on everyone's nerves, mostly his own. He had spearheaded premierships for Northcote in 1973–74 and 1974–75 and when Col Costorphin was picked ahead of him in the state squad he felt he was never going to get a run. Former wicketkeeper Ray Jordan suggested he move to South Australia because 'they haven't got any fast bowlers'.

Cosier, who Hogg called 'the jolly red giant', was excited at the possible move.

'I said to Ian, "There is a guy playing at Northcote and the moment he steps across the border he [becomes] the quickest guy in South Australia. He is a bit different but he is quick."'

While on an end-of-season footy trip to Adelaide Hogg stopped at Prospect Cricket Club and thought it looked like a good set-up. In his first match he took 5/35. He found wickets were a bit easier to gather in Adelaide than in Melbourne. His only issue was the different soil in the pitches. Hogg's action relied on jamming down on his front foot to create a whiplash effect and when it slipped his delivery rapidly lost speed.

The other problem was that there was another guy ahead of him, so Hogg went to see firsthand the work of Fang.

'There was a district game at the Adelaide Oval. West Torrens against Salisbury. Prior must have bowled 20 or 25 overs in a row of serious pace and with an outswinger. I have never seen a better bowler than him on his day.

'Prior, like a lot of people, played better under Chappell. Wayne was an easygoing bloke who needed Ian to get him going.'

Cosier believes that Hogg rated cricketers on their courage. If batsmen stood in there and didn't back away from him then he would have no problems with them – even honour them. They didn't have to be the best but they had to have guts.

This is why Hogg described playing for Chappell as an honour. He found himself a little starstruck when he walked out to play on the first day against Victoria.

'You did what he said. He didn't ask me anything, why would he? Some stuff captains say you don't pay attention to, but Ian might say the same thing but you listened – because it was Ian.'

Hogg's first wicket came in his first over and was straight from the textbook. A click as it passed Stillman's hooking bat, and a slap as Dennis Yagmich closed his gloves around it. Victoria 1/15.

With Ian Redpath missing with injury, Paul Hibbert and Graham Yallop took control, putting on 95 for the second wicket. Geoff Attenborough and Hogg bowled short and were punished. The batsmen played off the back foot and harvested a run a ball. At one stage Hibbert jumped from 13 to 31 in five scoring shots; square driving Hogg and pulling Attenborough to the fence. At lunch it was 1/101.

Chappell brought on Jenner after the break and in his first over he lured Hibbert into driving into the covers where Hookes snagged a brilliant catch. Incoming batsman Bob Baldry was on one when Jenner tricked him, but the chance was dropped by Chappell at slip. The Victorians capitalised with Yallop and Baldry, stepping up the tempo, adding 56 together in 49 minutes. Victoria 2/164.

Chappell made a double change bringing back Hogg and introducing Mallett. Two hours later Victoria were all out for 247 as an old dog and a young terrier swung the momentum, taking 7/94 between them and earning five bonus points while restricting Victoria to three.

Victoria's collapse began when Hogg had Yallop lbw when trying to force a ball through mid-wicket. When John Scholes came in, Chappell suggested Hogg avoid bowling at his legs because he was so strong there. The next over Hogg accidently strayed into his legs, Scholes clipped the ball to mid-wicket where Jenner bent low to pick off the catch.

The final wicket was that of Trevor Laughlin, hobbled with an infected foot, who belted Mallett to the square-leg boundary where Hookes raced, dived and came up with the ball. The mood in the South Australian rooms was buoyant. There was 45 minutes left to make a start.

Curtin prepared to go out, and put on a primitive thigh guard he referred to 'as about as useful as a copy of the *Women's Weekly*'. He struggled to keep his emotions under control as he walked out to open with Ashley Woodcock.

'As I walked through the gates with Splinter I naturally said to him, "You got it, mate", meaning you will take strike being senior. He said, "No, I don't do that" and [he] went to the other end.'

Curtin faced Alan Hurst. The first ball jagged back and squared him up. It flashed past his copy of the *Weekly*, nicked his back thigh and diverted to Richie Robinson at first slip. There was a muffled shout and Curtin prepared for the next ball only to see umpire Max O'Connell with his finger up.

'I didn't get anywhere near it. I thought that is great, first up. I finally get into the team again and am out first ball.'

Curtin was given an earful by one of the members on his trudge back to the rooms. It was still hot in the late afternoon and so he stripped off his gear, wrapped a towel around his waist and collapsed into a chair. Suddenly there was a commotion.

'Les Favell had been commentating in the ABC booth and [he] comes charging into the room shouting, "Where did that hit you? Where did that hit you?" "It didn't." "I know it didn't."'

Curtin pulled the towel off and together they examined a red seam mark on his thigh.

'Oh, bloody O'Connell,' howled Favell. 'He can't see – he is blind.'

Favell's exasperation grew when Woodcock was bowled by Bright for two with the total on 26. That was the stumps score. Sitting in the press box Keith Butler condensed the half-session for the next day's paper into three words: 'dominance to distress.'

*

Chappell was familiar with Victoria's new-ball attack of Max Walker and Hurst. Walker had been one of the heroes of the West Indies tour of 1973 and the following season it was Hurst that Chappell wanted in the Test side.

Australia was to tour New Zealand and Chappell was eager to find out who he would be leading. Rumours were sweeping around that both Keith Stackpole and Ian Redpath wouldn't be included in the touring party.

An irate Chappell fronted selector Sam Loxton who immediately began an impersonation of a sulphur-crested cockatoo, telling the captain that, 'We have dropped the whole bloody lot of you' before flying off. Chappell realised he had made a tactical error and after cooling down he contacted another selector, Neil Harvey. He confirmed both batsmen would be in the group but another Victorian wasn't included, which angered Chappell.

'I had said the only guy from New Zealand who can beat us is Glenn Turner, but Glenn doesn't like it when it is going past his nose. We had no Lillee and no Thomson, so Hurst is the only one with pace around. It was the only player I ever asked for while I was captain and I didn't get him. We lost one Test match in New Zealand and who got a hundred in each innings? Glenn Turner.'

The episode was part of the reason Chappell brokered a pact with South Australia's selectors that they inform him of any changes to the team. He didn't have a vote on who was picked but the written agreement was that he was to be told first of changes.

Walker and Hurst put a spear through South Australia's batting on the second day. In his second over Walker had Cosier (8) and Darling (1) both lbw. Hurst was peppering Chappell, a barrage that included a stinging blow on the hands. The spite grew.

'I said to Hurst, "You are pretty fucking brave when you are handing them out but you don't like them coming your way", or something like that. He bounced me and I hit it pretty well. He had a bat pad and as I hit it he yelled out "Catch it! Catch it!" I knew I had hit it for four but you jogged down anyway. As I jogged past him I said, "The only bloke who will catch it will be your bat pad and you will be responsible for his death if you keep bowling shit like that."

'Anyway, the next ball was perfect and got me lbw. He told me to fuck off or something. My theory, generally, is if you are out and someone tells you to piss off there is not much point in responding because you are out. However, on this occasion, for some reason I said, "Mate, I am on my way, but I will be back for a fucking second go.'"

The bravado in the face of South Australia's collapse drew amusement from the visiting side. The scoreboard was 5/54 and only a 32 from Hookes and 21 from Mallett added anything significant to the total of 146. Walker took 6/49 and Hurst 3/66. Victoria hadn't yielded a batting point but earned five bowling points and led by 101.

The swinging pendulum was now deep in the blue area, but for the rest of the day it crept gently back toward the red side of things. Mallett and Hogg took five wickets and Victoria was 147 at stumps. Hogg viewed Mallett as a 'different cat' but called him a superstar bowler because as a spinner he was capable of holding down an end or opening the bowling.

With the bonus points allocated, South Australia was atop the Shield table, eight points clear of Queensland. Both states had now played the same number of games. For Chappell the numbers didn't change anything. His side had a chance of taking the title in the last two games but an outright win here would almost do the job.

Victoria batted stubbornly to finish with 262 – a lead of 363. As he took off his pads in the South Australian rooms Yagmich listened to Jenner say that a total this high had only ever been overcome once before. He thought, "Okay, let's see what happens." He wasn't the only one who felt optimistic. Whether it was the success of the season, the improbably close wins or the belief generated by Chappell the side ignored the past two batting collapses and went for it.

Curtin remembers an unusually verbose captain.

'He said to the team, "They are not going to get me out today." It was rare to hear him say something like that. That game meant a lot to Ian. I had never seen him in such a fired-up mood. We knew if we won then we would be almost unbeatable for the Shield but it was a big ask. He had a thing for the Vics too. There was a lot of sledging, really tough.

'Ian's comment made me pumped and I thought, "We will get them." The track was still good – we would always go for 300 in a day because Ian would insist on that. He said to me that my technique is fine and he knew if I got a short ball early I would hit it for four and get on with it, whereas Drewer and Woodcock were similar types, they would just knock it down for six or seven overs.'

The score was 37 when Hurst bowled Woodcock. Chappell joined Curtin who was already flying. This was everything Curtin wanted from cricket. The risks he took came off and half his runs were coming from boundaries. Curtin liked the ball coming on to him, and Walker and Hurst were serving it up. In contrast, Chappell offered three chances which were all dropped. But they were chances from an aggressive bat. Twice Jim Higgs, near the square-leg fence, couldn't hang on to hook shots, and the third was a chance at backward-leg, dropped by Laughlin. Curtin started thinking differently about the captain's declaration about not getting out today, feeling perhaps it was a premonition about fielding not batting.

Curtin felt the game grew in quality with almost every ball. He was at the edge of his capacity finding gaps and running singles. But on 52 he leaned back to cut a ball from Bright and got a thick edge.

'Les Stillman at slip caught me and jagged it with two fingers. It was an incredible catch but that was what that game was like. I was spewing because I was batting with Ian and I really loved batting with him.'

Darling came in ahead of Cosier. It was a risky decision for a young batsman at a difficult time but he responded. Their unbeaten partnership of 83 left South Australia at 2/167 at stumps.

Before play on the final day, Chappell and Darling went to the nets to get their eye in. Chappell arranged for Prior to bowl to him and was pleased when the strike bowler said his ankle felt good. The two batsmen resumed in the middle and added only two runs when Darling played a loose shot to be caught behind off Hurst for 41.

After Cosier made 26 his dismissal triggered a mini-collapse. Hookes went for a duck and Jenner for 4. This left South Australia 6/225. The tension spilled over in Jenner's death walk. He slammed his bat into the back of a seat in the Members Stand, and again as he was about to enter the dressing room. A spectator shouted some advice to him and he turned and roared back, 'Shut your mouth or get out there your bloody self' before disappearing into the rooms.

It was now Chappell and the tail, and he cut loose. Twice he back-cut Hurst and then drove him through cover. He played leg-spinner Higgs off the back foot through cover. The fielders had no chance.

Mallett knew his role was to be resolute and he offered 105 minutes of company, gathering 19 as the score built to 288. During the partnership the antagonism between the sides grew – until it erupted.

The trouble had begun at the end of Victoria's second innings when Chappell told Attenborough to bowl short to Hurst. It was in retaliation for similar actions by Hurst against South Australia's tail.

Hurst hadn't forgotten. He was in his 14th over when he hit Mallett on the point of his shoulder. Mallett threw his bat up the wicket in anger. Chappell walked down and retrieved it and the pair talked as he returned the bat to Mallett.

During the next over from Hurst, Mallett was hit on his spinning finger, cracking a bone. He then leant forward to defend a delivery that reared up and hit him in the stomach and looped to Scholes who grabbed it at forward short-leg. The appeal was turned down. Mallett remembers Hurst threw the ball down in disgust.

'Ian walked over to the ball and hit it off the ground like a golf shot right down past his mark and said, "Not out, pal, now go and bloody get it."'

Mallett then gave Hurst the same treatment he had given Lillee, pulling away and asking for the immovable sightscreen to be adjusted. Hurst responded like Lillee, and the next ball hit Mallett on the upper arm. As the bat sailed 15 metres toward cover point, Chappell got involved.

'I thought, "I will put an end to this shit." Hurst had taken his cap from the umpire and was heading to fine-leg and I went with him and said, "Listen, you fucker, you bowl one more bouncer to Mallett and I will hit you over the head with this fucking bat. If you want to bounce anyone you bounce me." Hurst told me to get nicked or something. I suddenly thought, "Hang on, it's a bit crowded around here." And I looked and the two umpires [Max O'Connell and Tony Crafter] had got there. Max was saying "C'mon, Ian, settle down" and I said, "Don't worry, Max, it is all over. I wanted to get a message to this prick and I think he has got it." To his eternal discredit he didn't bounce Rowdy again and we put on 63 and that swung the game back in South Australia's favour.'

Hurst's defence – in bouncing Mallett –was that Mallett had been in for 45 minutes and should have been able to handle the short stuff. His captain, Richie Robinson, agreed adding that Hurst had been bounced by Attenborough and he was a number 11.

'In the heat of the moment and in the tight, critical period I think Hurst did the right thing,' Robinson said.

When Hurst took the new ball he immediately had Mallett caught behind. When Yagmich got to the crease South Australia still needed 75, while Victoria needed three wickets. The keeper could see that the marathon innings was starting to take its toll on Chappell. On fresh legs Yagmich sprinted for two and turned for a third. He was halfway down the pitch when he saw Chappell standing like an exhausted traffic cop with one hand in the air. He scrambled back in time and set about managing

182

the moments. For almost two hours Yagmich helped whittle the score down. Little was said between the batsmen and such was their concentration that they barely registered the bizarre timing of the ground announcer giving details of the South Australian side for its final two games in Sydney and Brisbane.

Yagmich and Chappell did not offer a chance in their 70-run partnership. Entering the final hour, when 15 overs were mandatory, the Victorians were wilting. Their attack was out of ideas. Hurst and Walker were spent but so was Chappell, and this was how they got him.

Jim Higgs was bowling and his flipper was so badly directed down the leg side it was almost a wide. Chappell went down on one knee to sweep the ball. He had to reach so far that in his exhausted state his bottom hand slipped off the bat and he was out, hit wicket.

Yagmich saw the ball disappear behind the keeper and he took off for a single – but then he spied the broken wicket.

'I looked into his face and said "Oh Christ" as if I was abusing him for getting out but I wasn't. It was just kind of my reaction to bad luck. I shouldn't have reacted that way but it was nerve-racking.'

After seven hours at the crease Chappell was out for 171. It was a brilliant knock – powerful, canny and enduring. Later he would describe it as the most satisfying Shield innings he ever played. South Australia now needed just five runs to win but Victoria needed the wickets of two bunnies. One of them crossed paths with Chappell on the field.

'Geoff Attenborough was coming in and I almost threatened him. I grabbed him and said, "Scatters, we have got to get these runs – make sure you get these runs." Geoff was a very good contributor to the team and he had a lot of self-confidence and he looked at me and said, "Don't worry, mate, we will get them."'

The four-day game that had waltzed slowly back and forth was now dancing on the head of a pin. Attenborough swept the first ball from Higgs for a single and that ended the over. He couldn't get behind the first ball from Walker which hit his bat and popped into the air, but fell safely between fielders. The next one snicked into the slips. Laughlin went for it but couldn't get all of it and his deflection went near Stillman who spilled it. Everyone exhaled then inhaled and held their breaths. Attenborough deflected a ball past Walker and scrambled through for a single. Yagmich blocked out the rest of the over.

Higgs, from the other end, looped one down which Attenborough accepted on one knee, coolly sweeping to the backward-leg boundary. Pandemonium erupted in the South Australian rooms. The batsmen walked off arm in arm and were engulfed by their team mates. Yagmich remembers it as one of the best moments of his life.

'As I sat down to take my pads off, Ian came over and put his hand on my head and said, "Yag, I am proud of you." I said thanks but the way he looked at me … he really meant that and it is something I will never forget until the day I die. It was really a touching moment for me because I don't think he said it too often but if you had done something well he would make that comment.'

The win meant the Shield could now be won on bonus points in the final two matches. The team of cast offs, kids and old blokes had beaten everyone. They made hasty plans to continue their celebrations at a North Adelaide pub.

Trouble was, no-one could find Chappell.

CHAPTER TEN

ON STRIKE

It would have been about the time that the SACA committee members were thinking about another drink that Chappell got to them. They had had a few blues in the past but nothing like this one. Chappell's crimson face was the result of both the three-and-a-half sessions he had spent out in the baking sun and the outrage that was now erupting.

Amid the yahooing in the rooms his mind had ticked back to the announcement over the tannoy that he had heard while out in the middle: details of South Australia's 'eastern tour' to play Queensland and New South Wales in its final two matches.

The announcer listed off the 13 names of the touring party including Bob Blewett, the captain-coach of East Torrens who was included for the first time. Thirteen names? That stuck in Chappell's mind. At this moment SACA secretary Darby Munn arrived.

'Poor old Darby was an inoffensive, lovely bloke but he happened to be the nearest administrator near me and so he caught my wrath.'

Munn was soon brushed aside as Chappell stormed out of the rooms and down the corridor into the committee room.

The selectors had done well. Hogg and Curtin had played significant roles in the victory. For the team's trip east they had decided to drop Drewer from the squad and add Blewett. The 32-year-old heard the news from a friend who rang and woke him at seven in the morning. Blewett found it hard to believe that after so long he had been called up. He was about to turn 33 and was six months older than Chappell. He went to work that day at the Savings Bank of South Australia keeping an ear on the radio for updates on the extraordinary events unfolding at the Adelaide Oval.

Chappell had been a fierce rival of Blewett's in district cricket but had no gripes about him being selected. His anger was because the selectors had breached the agreement that they would notify him in advance of any changes.

The decision to pick Blewett had been made on Sunday and when Chappell phoned Ridings that night he was told it was a cover for Prior. Chappell knew Prior had bowled well to Cosier in the nets that day and asked Ridings to take a look at Prior in the nets Monday morning. Ridings said it was too late.

Chappell demanded to know why he hadn't been consulted; he was told they couldn't because he was out batting at the time.

'I thought that was my fucking job,' he shouted.

When he demanded to know why Drewer was dropped, he was told that it was because he couldn't play fast bowling.

'Hang on, he has had a problem with Lillee. I don't know if you have noticed but a lot of other batsmen around the world who are better players at Test level have had problems with Lillee,' he said.

'Have a look at Drewer's average against New South Wales. He averages 40 opening the batting. He carves them up, especially Gilmour. If we get a start in Sydney and get plenty of bonus points then we win the Shield.'

Chappell felt loyal to Drewer. If things went well this was going to be a celebration tour and his stumpy opener deserved to enjoy the party having played the whole season. He also resented the committee splashing out for airfares and accommodation for an unnecessary 13th player when they wouldn't even pay for the players' laundry bills while they were away. Even the cost of cleaning their whites had to be covered by the players.

'If you are going to spend the extra money for a 13th man, then don't,' he said. 'Spend it on the guys who have played their backside off to get us here instead.'

Both parties were exasperated. Exhausted from batting and bewildered by administration, Chappell quit. It was all he could think of doing. He had delivered the improbable, bringing a side considered the weakest in Australia to the verge of being the strongest. He had created the environment and stood up to bullies and most significantly had led from the front – including the 171 against Victoria that Richie Benaud called 'one of the most exciting performances … in 25 years'. Along the way he felt unsupported and misunderstood by administrators. So to hell with them.

The first person he told was Mallett, explaining to his old campaign mate what had happened and that he wouldn't be going to Sydney and Brisbane.

'If you are not going then I am not going,' said Rowdy.

Jenner also decided not to go but he wanted to take it further. He called a team meeting and cleared the room. Drewer, as 12th man, stayed but Nugget Rees left. Any journos, parents or backslappers were booted out. Curtin remembers Bradman being among those ushered hastily away.

Once it was just the players the pace settled. Their meeting went for an hour and a half. Jenner took control by saying that because he worked for Coca-Cola, which was a SACA sponsor, he could act as a go-between. He got Chappell to explain what happened.

According to Hookes, Chappell said the decision was a personal one and shouldn't affect the others but Jenner disagreed, arguing that if it was good enough for the captain not to go on tour then it is good enough for the rest of the team. Mallett agreed. Curtin could see Chappell was still emotional and understood why.

'He always seemed to be bashing his head against a wall with the SACA and never got anything he wanted,' says Curtin. 'They didn't like him. [I felt that] I am part of the team [and] if that is how we are going [striking] then let's do it.'

Drewer's emotions were torn. He was suffering a bruised ego at being dropped but felt complimented that he was still considered part of the team. It confirmed to him what he already sensed – that the side had grown incredibly tight over the season.

Jenner proposed a vote as to whether or not they would join Chappell. Pieces of paper were found. Chappell and Drewer abstained from the secret ballot. When the score was tallied it was 8–2 in support of the captain. Jenner said it couldn't be a split result, that it was all in or all out. The only person out at this stage was Chappell who excused himself from the room so his presence didn't affect anyone.

Cosier and Hogg voted against the idea. Hogg felt there was a gap between the senior players, who had already had long first-class careers, and those aspiring to them.

'I thought the strike was a bit selfish of the senior players. Hookes and Darling were just starting out. They may have had old gripes with the board but it hurt the young players.'

Yagmich was stunned. The moment of ecstasy after the game had soured so quickly. When Jenner asked him what his thoughts were he said he felt Drewer had been unfairly treated after grafting and grinding all season. He also felt loyalty to Chappell.

'I said that after what Ian has done for us we shouldn't go to Sydney without him. I thought this might be the end of my cricket career.'

Prior felt the same. 'We were always going to back Ian. Whatever he wanted we would have done. I remember Nugget Rees came into the rooms and he was breaking down crying.'

After a long discussion, Jenner called for another vote.

'I pushed a little bit, suggesting we should think about ourselves as a team and the future,' Jenner said.

This time it was unanimous. The strike was on. Lighting up a fag, Curtin joked that having finally got back into the South Australian team he had voted himself out of it. Hogg agreed with the irony.

Jenner told Ridings and Favell that the players supported Chappell and that if he didn't go then they wouldn't either. Then things escalated. While Jenner negotiated with the irate administrators, many of the players continued the discussion at a more agreeable venue. It was now late in the evening as they drifted towards the Old Lion Hotel. Hookes remembered his girlfriend, Roxanne, had been waiting for him.

'We were supposed to be going out to dinner at seven o'clock. Now it is about twenty to ten and she is still waiting under the John Creswell Stand at the Adelaide Oval. We had the first of many blues because she just thought I was in there drinking Southwark for three hours.'

Jenner was the last to leave the empty oval. The note of defiance signed by all the players sat smouldering in the hands of the administrators. The players' discussion at the bar turned to what price might be paid for backing Chappell.

By the time Jenner arrived at the pub most players had gone home. He decided to have a couple of drinks with the last few, and then go to the pie cart for dinner. After four days of tense cricket, and a night of impromptu industrial action, he ordered champagne and it went down like cordial. He stayed until everyone had left and then got into his work car with the Coca-Cola livery and drove around the corner – where he was stopped by police and done for drink-driving.

*

Mutinies in Australian cricket have traditionally ended heavily in favour of the establishment. In 1912 a group of six senior Australian players boycotted a tour of England after they were denied their preferred team manager by the board, which had selected its own man. The conflict was actually over money because it was the manager who sorted out how the financial cake was cut (including gate receipts) and so the players feared, rightly, that the board's preferred choice would have short arms and deep pockets.

The half dozen dissenters were the biggest names in the sport – Victor Trumper, Clem Hill, Warwick Armstrong, Tibby Cotter, Hanson Carter and Vernon Ransford. It didn't matter. Despite having popular opinion on their side, the players lost out. The board picked a new captain and half a new side. On the tour the team played badly on and off the field but the board had imposed its control over money and managerial appointments for all future tours.

When Bill Lawry led the Australians through India in 1969 he reached the end of his tether with the demanding schedule. The players were crook from the food and struggling in the basic accommodation. Lawry called them together for one long vent, which he recorded. He then put together a dossier of complaints for the board in the hope they would consult more on future campaigns. Chappell suggested to Lawry that the entire touring party sign the letter in a show of unity. Lawry disagreed, believing it was his role as captain to take the lead.

Many believe the letter was the reason Lawry was sacked as captain the following home summer when his form started to fade. He heard the news on the radio, and not from chairman of selectors, Don Bradman. Chappell considered the act one the most insensitive things he had seen in cricket, and the circumstances under which he got the job are the reason he told his wife 'the bastards will never get me like that'.

So when word reached Bradman at his Kensington home on Monday evening that Chappell was refusing to play, and the others were going out in sympathy, he backed the authority of the selectors.

'No one man can insist on one particular player just because it suits his fancy,' he said.

By now Ridings was at his home working from a rumpus room he had built on the back of his house. He described the team as irresponsible and their actions as a humiliating blow to South Australia.

'They have shown scant respect for the interests of cricket in this state, especially with SA in such a strong position to win the Shield.'

Ridings then got on the front foot. On behalf of the administrators he sent a message to Jenner that anyone wanting to make themselves available for the eastern states tour had to do so by midday on Tuesday otherwise a new state side and captain would be selected.

*

The players copped a hammering in the press. Editorials called them 'sad and silly' and 'flannelled fools' and their strike a 'massive over-reaction' and a 'farce'. Moreover, according to the press, the blame was with Chappell whose 'contribution to the game has been sadly diminished recently by the example he has set of needlessly brash behaviour'. The players, it was said, suffered from 'mistaken loyalty'.

Benaud expressed respect for Chappell and the three selectors but not the standoff.

'In their own fields in life they are top men. How they could have allowed South Australian cricket to arrive at this stage, even allowing for militancy of current players and the conservatism of administrators, is beyond me.'

A newspaper cartoon lampooning the strike depicted two children playing street cricket. A small boy is batting and looks at a baby with a dummy in its mouth. The caption read: 'Let's play Sheffield Shield … you can be South Australia.' A dog in the corner mutters: 'Play up, Play up, Boycott the game.'

Hookes was about to have breakfast on Tuesday morning when the phone rang. It was Attenborough.

'Have you seen the paper?' he started.

Attenborough stayed on the line while Hookes retrieved the paper from the front lawn. Underneath the masthead, spread across the front page, were mug shots of all 12 players over a headline: 'STATE CRICKETERS QUIT'.

Hookes got back on the phone to Scatters who asked, 'What do you think we are going to do?'

'I think we are going on strike.'

The scene was repeated at homes and workplaces. Curtin slipped into work at Wesfarmers and tried to keep a low profile. They had agreed not talk to anyone about what was happening and he knew his boss was a cricket nut and would be looking for the inside word.

Yagmich sat staring at the ledgers he should have been auditing but was sweating bullets while hoping the phone would ring with someone telling him what was happening.

Among the things Jenner had to explain was why he couldn't drive the company car to work.

Before he hung up Attenborough suggested to Hookes they see Chappell and so they drove to his home. Chappell urged them to make themselves available.

'Ian said, "I am ending my career and you are just starting so there is no way you should go down this track if you don't want to. It won't mean anything to me, I will speak to TJ and you can withdraw from the strike." I said no, we are happy,' said Hookes.

Blewett rang, offering to withdraw from the squad. Chappell told him not to but the offer softened him. Woodcock arrived shortly after Mallett. Mallett was steadfast in his support for

Chappell but Woodcock turned the argument around. He explained that the team had backed their captain in his protest after the Victoria game and now they wanted Chappell to back them by returning.

Woodcock had been the one who arranged a pre-season weekend in the Adelaide Hills to build camaraderie and skills. He reminded Chappell of how long the season had been.

'My pitch to Ian was, "Let's go away, win it to stick it up them, and then deal with it. We need you as captain to lead the way."'

Chappell had rung the other players encouraging them to make themselves available but they remained stubbornly loyal to him. He was stuck because he couldn't imagine going back on his threat. The phone call that finally changed his mind came from someone outside cricket.

Neil Kerley was the Ian Chappell of South Australian football – tough, talented and resourceful. He had two nicknames. The first was 'Knuckles' because his hands had been so badly damaged during play that they were swollen into unnatural settings. The second was 'The King' because of his dominance of the game. He loved challenges, relished contests and arced up against authority. As a result he had moved from club to club but the result was the same at each one – success. He won premierships as a captain and coach and did it with both his chin and his chest poking out. His original club was West Adelaide, the side Chappell barracked for. When Chappell answered the phone he heard Kerley's distinctive growl urging him to play.

Kerley's half-order, half-appeal, came with the rare context of someone who understood the effort needed to lead South Australia against stronger states. Kerley never felt inferior to anyone but he played with those who did. He had lost many more contests against Victoria and Western Australia than he had won so he knew what was at stake here.

Chappell acceded to 'The King'. Woodcock agreed to make the calls.

An ABC television crew was waiting outside. Chappell went to see them but looked downcast. He wore a purple paisley body shirt and, rather than stand, leant forward resting his arms on the fence. He explained his decision in a low voice.

'I don't play for the SACA any more, I am just playing for those other XI.'

'You will be South Australian captain?'

'Only for the next two games.'

'What beyond that?'

'At this stage I couldn't see myself staying on as captain. They haven't got the faith in my captaincy to consult me on the selection of the team. I can't see that there is any point me staying in the job.'

'But you have brought South Australia to the verge of the Sheffield Shield.'

'I haven't done that, the team has done that. A captain is only as good as his team. It is the team that has probably got me to go to Sydney and Brisbane. The fact that these fellows have put in so much effort this season … I guess I would have been very selfish if I had said, well, out the window with that effort.'

'Should anything be done to the SACA to improve relations?'

'I have been trying to push a bit and they feel I am impatient. This is the reason I said I wouldn't go because I am sick of being pushed around. As far as I am concerned I am sick of talking – this was my action. I always believe actions speak louder than words. I am not talking any longer. As far as I am concerned they can sort the problem out for themselves.'

*

In the minutes before midday, Darby Munn put down the phone and checked the list again. The players had all agreed to go. There were 13 names including Blewett, but not Drewer.

The actions of the 12 would result in disciplinary action to be decided at a meeting of the SACA in a fortnight. Ridings echoed Bradman's statement that the opinion of one man to dictate to them would never be allowed.

Bradman made no further public comment on the industrial action, although he did privately. He was a correspondent and among those he regularly exchanged letters with was the English cricket writer EW Swanton. Decades later, Australian cricket publisher Ron Cardwell got hold of the letters the pair exchanged and included was a reference to the events of 1975–76.

Swanton wrote asking Bradman about Wayne Prior's suitability for a stint with county side Kent. Bradman's response was: 'Properly handled I don't think he would be a troublemaker.'

He continued: 'He was in the Chappell "revolt" but I shall always believe they were conned into that by the mastermind.

The young players in the SA team were brainwashed by Chappell and the next morning they were all prepared to smartly reverse their decision (which in fact they did) when they found out their careers were finished if they went on with it. I believe Chappell persuaded them that the selectors would back down but for once Chappell over-played his hand and fell in a hole.'

The letter leaves Chappell cold.

'Interesting that in many communications with Bradman – not just mine but also others – people were castigated for assuming things about Bradman. However, he's quite happy to assume a couple of things in this situation, all of which were wrong.

'Bradman pisses me off. If he was still alive I would tell him there are other ways to get players to play for you than brainwash them. [That] might have been his way but it wasn't mine.'

CHAPTER ELEVEN

IN REACH OF THE TITLE

New South Wales v. South Australia,
Sydney, February 27–March 2, 1976

Queensland v. South Australia, Brisbane, March 5–8, 1976

The Sydney hill lived up to its reputation for wit as Chappell went out to bat late on the first day of the Shield match against New South Wales. Doug Walters had recovered from his knee injury and, after winning the toss, had chosen to bat. The return of Walters had inspired consecutive victories over Victoria and Western Australia, the latter scuppering Western Australia's slim title chance. Walters made a sharp 50 before Prior – who ended up with five wickets – had him caught behind. Gary Gilmour pounded out 80 in a total of 238. The home side had three batting points but more significantly South Australia claimed five bowling points.

Now batting, the visitors lost Ashley Woodcock, caught behind off Len Pascoe for three with the total on five. Chappell walked down the path and through the gate and, in perfect comic timing, as his leading foot touched the turf, a voice yelled: 'I thought it was one out all out.' Chappell laughed all the way to the crease.

It was a welcome break from the tension that had followed the team. There had been a certain sense of relief for the players as their Sydney-bound plane lifted off on Wednesday morning. By coincidence, Premier Don Dunstan was on the flight and sitting close by.

'G'day Don,' chirped Terry Jenner, 'Up for the game are you?'

Dunstan explained that he was heading to Canberra for a wine conference but he wished the team luck.

Before Jenner found his seat he spotted Bob Blewett and said in an angry tone: 'I won't be bowling to you at practice – and don't you expect to bowl to me, Woodcock or Yagmich.'

An uncomfortable silence fell over the group before Blewett asked why.

'Kensington plays East Torrens in the last game [of grade cricket] and we don't want you working out our weaknesses,' he said, to the relief of the players around who caught onto his mock indignation.

The flight was a brief interlude before they faced the music again. As they waited at the Sydney terminal to catch a bus to the motel, baggage handlers asked: 'If we don't load you boys, you won't have a stop-work meeting will you?'

Old district war stories were a common theme at dinner that evening in a restaurant near their motel, and if anything the group felt even closer than they had all season. Although they were disparate in age and personality, the players all later regarded the side as communal in nature.

The morning newspapers that slid under their doors further added to the us-versus-them feeling.

One paper described the South Australians as a 'swearing, swaggering lot' while reprinting comments from *London Evening News* scribe Doug Ibbotson who backed the establishment, hoping the episode 'should speed the arrogant, hard-swearing and ungracious Chappell into permanent retirement'.

In another paper New South Wales batsman Peter Toohey claimed he had been taunted by South Australian fielders while batting at the Adelaide Oval. He was quoted saying he had never experienced such ill-feeling and threatened to square up.

'If this is what first-class cricket is all about I would rather go back and play in the bush. If there is any bullying to be done out there, I'll be doing it with the bat.'

Walters re-enforced the sentiment saying, 'If the South Australians want to carry on with their tantrums and antics then let them.'

The press arrived en masse at South Australia's net session later in the morning. Chappell was ready for them. With cameras whirring he explained, with a smile on his face, his actions of the past few days and then said, 'Let's get down to those accusations of swearing, swaggering and tantrums.'

'It appears that someone around here doesn't like us being on top of the Shield table. Of course we play it tough but what happens out there on the field does not go any further. I have the youngest side in the competition and most of my players would not say boo to a goose.'

His tone then darkened as he addressed comments that there was no love lost between him and Greg.

'I don't mind talking to any of you but I don't want to be misquoted. I said there was no love lost between Greg and myself when we were on opposite sides on the field. I repeat for you – on the cricket field. Off the field we all have a drink together. So next time, would you mind getting your facts right.'

The press pack placated, the team practised except for Wayne Prior who only gently rolled his arm over. There was no-one to tape his ankle and so Chappell refused to risk him taking any more than a few paces. The following morning with his ankle taped Prior bowled well in the nets and replied positively to Chappell's query about his fitness. Although Rodney Hogg had been spectacular against Victoria he was named 12th man with Attenborough selected in his stead. Blewett was 13th man.

Blewett was sharing a room with David Hookes who had lost a bet over his selection. Rick Drewer had wagered a bottle of red that he wouldn't be in the 13-man touring party and now Hookes had to pay up. Back in Adelaide, Drewer announced his retirement from first-class cricket. He said the decision wasn't because he was dropped (although he expressed disappointment about that) but that he intended travelling to China to study politics and history and complete a teaching degree.

What no-one knew was the impact the tumultuous week would have on the team. Richie Benaud worried about it in his column. He described South Australia's off-field fortunes as being at the lowest ebb of any state he could recall and he referenced the 1912 ruckus as the only parallel. He suggested the team now had to play like hell to win the Shield.

'But there is a second possibility – the reaction from the tempestuous events of Tuesday could see them disintegrate and at this stage I wouldn't like to bet on either.'

The bet looked like it was going against the visitors as Prior opened with his worst over of the season. In hot and muggy conditions, but with a useful breeze behind him, Fang sprayed his first ball down the leg side for four wides. His line and length were all over the place and two full tosses were put away by McCosker. The over cost eleven. Prior was hooted by those on the hill and eventually gave them a two-fingered reply. It was the only response from the fielders to the niggling comments that floated in the sultry air all day.

Prior's second over wasn't as expensive but it was far from glamorous. His control returned in the third when a stunning delivery jagged back from outside the off side, clipped the edge of Alan Turner's bat and sent the leg stump rocketing out of the ground.

At the start of his third over Attenborough slipped and strained his left side. After several balls he felt worse and left the field. Gary Cosier took over from his end from where he bowled

Rick McCosker for 34. Toohey was trapped lbw by Jenner for four. Several dropped catches helped the home side and they grew in confidence, with Gilmour especially in a dangerous mood. He added 105 in partnership with Graeme Hughes.

Then they collapsed, losing 6/27 to be all out for 238. At one stage Mallett took 2/2 in seven balls but it was Prior who again torched the tail. In his 13th over he took wickets with the third, seventh and eighth balls – leaving him on a course for another hat-trick with the first ball of the next innings.

South Australia's reply began disastrously when Woodcock fell to Pascoe for 3, after nicking behind to wicketkeeper Steve Rixon. With his team 1/5 Chappell found himself in the middle much earlier than he would have liked. Once Chappell had gained his focus he pushed the total to 41. His old antagonist Pascoe bounced him, a delivery Chappell pulled through mid-on where David Hourn tried to snag it. He managed to get a finger to it but succeeded only in deflecting the ball into his face, almost concussing him. In the final over it was Curtin who seemed to have a brain fade. He swung at a wild delivery from David Colley that was heading about a foot over his head. The contact he made knocked the ball to Pascoe who was fielding at backward leg.

Curtin recalls his captain's voice, succinctly expressing his frustration at losing a wicket at such a vital time: 'You fucking Port Adelaide c***.'

Yagmich came in as night watchman and at stumps South Australia was 2/46. Curtin had thrown down his gear and sat in the rooms in despair. When Chappell sat next to him he prepared for a blast but instead a cooler voice said, 'I don't care about getting out but do not stop hooking – do not stop hooking – you will get more runs than you will get out.'

The team searched for news from Brisbane. They were delighted when they heard that Western Australia had won the toss and that openers Laird (119) and Charlesworth (61) had taken control. The visitors were 6/230 at stumps.

Greg Chappell calculated that he would only get a few batting points and so needed an outright win over Western Australia, and for New South Wales to defeat South Australia. That would set up the final match of the summer at the Gabba as the competition decider. Two things stood in his way: forecast rain and his older brother.

*

The rain held off but Ian didn't. For the second time in six days he played a brilliant innings under intense pressure. Such was his single-mindedness that when he reached three figures he didn't acknowledge the applauding crowd. Instead, he hitched up his strides, adjusted his pads and marked his crease out again. Alan Shiell described it as 'an unforgettable, grimly determined hand of almost inestimable value'. Keith Butler wrote that his 'rugged defiance and skill [had] lifted his team of rebels from a desperate plight to one of strength'. Walters called it 'typical Ian'.

It took 237 minutes and included 13 boundaries on heavy turf. There was history in it too because the runs saw him become

South Australia's second-highest all-time run-scorer – passing the rebellious Clem Hill to almost touch Les Favell.

More importantly, however, Chappell's runs made Shield success more likely. There was victory too over the bosses, the snobs, the critics and the knuckleheads. He was the captain and he did was captains do – he led.

As Chappell compiled that century his team mates struggled under the pressure. Yagmich was sent back in the first over of the day after being caught short while risking a third run. Rick Darling, flattened by a chest infection, struggled for 12 in 43 minutes before going lbw. Cosier was out of sorts and needed almost half an hour to find his first run. He was caught behind off a poor cut shot for 14. South Australia reeled at 5/102.

Hookes – the Chappell acolyte – helped provide the key partnership. Together they made 88 in 104 minutes. Although Hookes scored only 24 he batted perfectly in rhythm with Chappell. Then he tried flicking Kerry O'Keeffe, striking a flamingo pose with his back foot lifted above the crease. He missed but wicketkeeper Rixon didn't. The score was now 6/190.

After ten more runs were added darkness ended play and soon the heavens opened. It was 40 minutes before tea but play was soon abandoned as the SCG became a lake. Watching from the dressing room as the rain fell the players made the calculations. They now had two batting points (plus the five bowling points) and another 13.4 overs to gain the 50 runs needed to earn two more. South Australia now had 101 points and Queensland 78.

The reports from Brisbane were encouraging. The Western Australian tail had wagged adding 90 runs for a first innings total of 320. Greg Chappell had become increasingly frustrated as Marsh's team batted for 92.4 overs. The last wicket to fall was Mick Malone who, while going for a sharp single, collided with Chappell who was trying to field the ball off his own bowling. Davis gathered it and threw down the stumps but it was a long, agonising wait before umpire Mick Harvey raised his finger. Malone was irate. Queensland threw the bat at everything and was 2/91 when the rain began falling in enormous drops.

The rain fell all night and day in Brisbane. It washed out Sunday, leaving Queensland only one day to seek an outright win. The South Australians watched the title fall into their laps without them lifting a finger. The SCG didn't allow Shield games played on Sunday and so they spent the day lounging around the motel, never having been so excited by meteorological reports. The centre of attention was a tropical low that had brewed in the Solomon Sea east of Papua New Guinea and was making its way south. As it did it gained strength and was classified as a category three tropical cyclone named Colin. Its winds whipped up waves that pounded the beaches of southern Queensland. Swells of up to 12 metres were recorded off Sydney Heads, and there were two metre swells inside Botany Bay. Curtin suggested to team manager Colin Grant that South Australia forfeit the game to Queensland and spend the four days celebrating in Surfers Paradise.

Chappell remained resolute, figuring out how things could be taken care of by his team rather than relying on others. If they scored at a run per ball on Monday they could reach 275 and gain three batting points.

They only got two. Chappell was caught by Gilmour off Hourn for 119 while Jenner was unbeaten on 34. The total was 7/250 when Chappell declared the innings – one ball short of 65 overs. New South Wales was 2/39 when rain ended play.

The news from the north was that Colin had done the damage. The game was abandoned due to a waterlogged pitch and surrounds. Queensland took only two points from the match and was now 25 points adrift of South Australia.

Chappell sat in the SCG rooms reading the paper as the rain fell. It wouldn't stop for days. Around him the team remained low-key, making him believe that winning the Sheffield Shield had not sunk in. They were still in game mode. Geoff Attenborough had more treatment for his injured side, some players read while others tossed a ball around. The only thing being drunk was tea.

Chappell told reporters there was no reason to start celebrating because the season wasn't over until the final game was played. He then smirked as he explained that he had worked out that if his side didn't beat New South Wales outright, Queensland could still tie with them.

'All they have to do is to score 400 in 65 overs, get us out without our scoring a batting point, and win outright.'

His competitive nature and respect for his sibling meant he regretted the way the season was fagging out.

'It looked like building into a climax in Brisbane this week but it's now something of a letdown for Greg. It has been a great year [for South Australia]. As I hoped before the season began we played our matches at our top for four days, not two as we have done in recent seasons. There was a tremendous team spirit and the arrival of several young batsmen gave us more solidity.'

The following day the players all made their way back to the ground for the sake of formality. It had rained all night and was still coming down. When the match was officially abandoned Colin Grant took a phone call from Adelaide. He returned to the rooms to tell the team the SACA had told him to put $50 on the bar to celebrate.

He was met with derision – the players treating the announcement as if it were a gag. Keith Butler from the *Advertiser* pointed out that this might be their only prize from winning the Sheffield Shield. The players expressed a belief that the SACA may fine them as a group for their attempted mutiny and that could involve withholding any extra payments. The tone darkened when they returned to the topic of a lack of superannuation, incentives or sponsorship compared with other states. The only financial bonus being offered for the team had come from an incentive fund. A total of almost $4,300 had been raised from sponsors including a local builder, winery and car tyre dealership.

When news reached Adelaide of the reaction, Darby Munn explained that the $50 was a spontaneous gesture rather than a formal recognition of the team's Shield victory. That would require a decision of the ground and finance committee or the cricket committee.

'Although we appear certain to have won the Shield, it is premature to celebrate it officially before the final match of the season is over.'

*

The rain was easing as the South Australians arrived in Brisbane. The Gabba was such a quagmire that Greg Chappell suggested finding another ground, but the Queensland Cricket Association insisted the venue be used. The ground was heavy and the pitch underprepared and grassy. When Ian Chappell won the toss he didn't hesitate to send Queensland in to bat rather than face Jeff Thomson on a green top.

South Australia included Hogg and Blewett in the XI, after Attenborough's injury against New South Wales, and after Darling twisted his ankle slipping on a flight of stairs in the Sydney Motel on Tuesday evening.

Under heavy skies Queensland's openers went out to face the pace. With Prior and Hogg bowling the innings wasn't expected to last long but Queensland's top five all made runs and the home side kept the scoreboard ticking over as it reached 7/348 (six batting points) off 70 overs.

Greg Chappell played the ball elegantly to all corners and shared a 119-run partnership with David Ogilvie. Chappell's 79 in 82 minutes belied the conditions. With the quick bowlers posing no threat, Mallett was brought on. He thought he had an instant result when he appealed loudly for an lbw.

'Mick Harvey was the umpire and Greg was plum,' says Mallett. 'He was given not out so I thought "bugger this" and so just threw up junk with the attitude of "hit that, then". This was pretty stupid because he did just that and took 28 off the over.'

The explosive innings also pushed Greg (1547) within range of Bradman's best season of 1690 runs. But the tail of Cyclone Colin flicked overnight and while the umpires hoped a break in the weather would allow play to start again on the second day it didn't. Nor was there any play on days three and four.

So the season that had begun in spring with a prediction no-one had much confidence in, and which gained momentum during summer through a series of improbably daring raids on better-stocked teams, ended in autumn with two umpires standing grimly in the rain, their ankles sinking into the Gabba turf, declaring that the elements had won. The match was drawn and South Australia were officially Shield champions.

South Australia finished the Shield season with 105 points ahead of Queensland on 84. Western Australia had humiliated Victoria in two days at the MCG in their final game to finish third with 78, followed by New South Wales on 71, and Victoria on 60.

If the Queensland game was an anti-climax the party wasn't. It took place in Curtin's room with Chappell making the arrangements. The team was staying at the Gazebo Hotel at Spring Hill across the river from the Gabba and Curtin's was the top room.

'Ian was on the phone to mobs like the Brothers Rugby Club [asking for] this or that. Everyone was there. It was one of the great nights of my life. Everything happened – many funny things, and a few weird things. That was a wild, wild night after we won the Shield.'

At one stage Chappell remembered that they needed a refrigerator moved. He assumed it was full of booze. As he was trying to coordinate a couple of guys to shift it, Prior picked it up in a bear hug and single-handedly moved it to the astonishment of his captain.

'I always thought Fang was a strong bugger but I just didn't realise how strong he was until he just picked the bloody thing up and moved it himself.'

As Chappell led the players past midnight, back in Adelaide delegates from each of the district clubs gathered to discuss the team's actions. After two hours it decided on a sub-committee to investigate what had taken place after the game against Victoria by interviewing every player. Their investigation wouldn't happen in a hurry because Chappell and Mallett were heading to South Africa for an exhibition double wicket competition and the decision was to talk to them when they returned.

At the highest level, however, the outcome was seen as a formality. Earlier in the week, as the game at the Gabba was starting, an emergency meeting of the SACA committee had decided the players would be severely reprimanded on their return from Brisbane and that Chappell would be sacked for disloyalty. Legal advice had been sought.

The hungover team members were met at the airport by cricket committee chairman Dick Niehuus and Darby Munn.

They were told to report to the SACA the following afternoon. When they did they were surprised to see Chappell. He had delayed his trip long enough to be there. He didn't like the idea of the young players going in on their own, insisting they have a senior member with them. So the players went in groups – first Mallett, Cosier and Curtin, then Jenner, Yagmich, Darling and Prior, and finally Woodcock, Attenborough, Hookes and Chappell. Hogg was in Melbourne.

Hookes remembered things getting off to an awkward start when Ridings called him by his father's name, Russell.

When the meetings ended Niehuus said it was apparent the players regretted the way the incident developed and that it was made clear the committee deplored the action taken.

'This was considered to be quite unjustified and reflected no credit on them,' he said.

Chappell hurried out saying he had no regrets and 'one thing that was achieved tonight was that all the players met members of the committee. Hopefully this augurs well for the future – that is the main concern.'

Once he was gone it was Jenner who again acted as group spokesman. In a conciliatory tone he said he thought they all regretted what had happened and understood they couldn't dictate to the selectors. However, he finished with this: 'Perhaps all of us didn't believe in the intensity of every point Chappell made, and perhaps we didn't agree on every point, but the respect for Chappell is so great that we could not consider touring without him.'

The next time the team was all together again it was with 180 guests at a dinner thrown by department store tycoon Sir Edward Hayward at his John Martin's Buttery cafeteria in Rundle Street. Speeches were made and the incentive fund cheque was presented to Chappell by Ridings. The State Savings Bank added $10 for every catch taken, giving Yagmich a handy $300 for the season.

The planned sanctions faded with the SACA deciding that given the length of time the matter should now be dropped. The season had been a financial bonanza and at its AGM a profit of $104,760 was announced – above the $84,495 of the previous Ashes summer. Instead of showing him the door, the SACA awarded Ian Chappell life membership for having given long service to South Australia, noting that recent problems should be set aside.

It added: He was an extremely successful captain and a great leader who had the ability to gain and hold loyalty among his team mates.

*

Although Greg Chappell's perfect season was ruined by his brother there was some redress. The sparkling innings Greg played on the first day of the meaningless final game earned him three umpires' votes for the cricketer-of-the-year award. Ian didn't have a chance to bat and thus earn any votes himself.

Those three votes meant that the brothers tied for the title and had to split the $1,000 prize. Ian finished the season with 840 runs at 76.36 while Greg had 800 at 80. The next best batsman was McCosker with 526 at 52.60. The Chappells both had 25 votes from the umpires. Then came Prior (15), Lillee (14), Thomson and Gilmour (12 each).

Mallett led all bowlers with 38 wickets, followed by Lillee with 35, Prior and Thomson with 33, and Hurst with 32.

After the award was announced the brothers were on the phone offering mutual congratulations. Late in the conversation Greg paused and asked: 'Ian, how the hell did you guys win the Sheffield Shield?'

EPILOGUE

David Hookes attracted an enormous crowd for his final appearance at the Adelaide Oval. The line into the ground snaked around the car park and on to War Memorial Drive. Flowers were placed on the seat in the grandstand where his mother, Pat, had preferred watching him play. In the middle of the ground his bat rested against the stumps, with his red South Australian cap hanging on the handle. This is how Hookes used to leave his gear during breaks when he batted – signalling an ownership of the centre square with the idea that while he was away for a moment, he would be back for more soon. The members of the 1975–76 Shield side came to mourn. Chappell spoke. It was 27 January 2004. He started with a gentle nod to anti-establishment sentiments: 'Hookesy, I knew you wouldn't like me to wear a tie today so I haven't let you down.'

The day before, Chappell agreed to be interviewed about the sudden and wrenching loss of Hookes who had died a week earlier. Hookes was coaching Victoria and, after a match against South Australia, the teams had gone to a pub in St Kilda. There had been an argument with security staff and words were exchanged followed by punches. A bouncer connected with him once outside the pub. Hookes fell backwards onto the road and never regained consciousness. He was taken off life support the next day. The man who threw the fatal punch, Zdravko Micevic, was acquitted of manslaughter a year later.

Hookes was 48 and had been living in Melbourne for several years to further his media career. His shift into coaching had been seamless, reviving Victoria's fortunes and winning the Sheffield Shield in his second season in charge. Now he was gone.

Australia was playing a one-day match against Zimbabwe in front of an Australia Day holiday crowd. During a break in his commentary duties with Channel Nine, Chappell found a quiet spot to speak about how the pickets at the ground at mid-wicket and extra-cover had been bruised over the years by Hookes. But the dashing play wasn't his primary memory.

'I think the thing about him I will always remember is as a bloke. He liked to have a good time and even if it was just a conversation over a beer at the end of a day's commentary, or whatever, he liked it to be interesting. I think half the time that is why he would lob a hand grenade in halfway through the conversation, just to liven things up a little bit.'

In 1975–76 Hookes and Rick Darling had been the young wonders who gave the South Australian side enthusiastic fielding and late-order runs. While Darling was reserved socially, Hookes was, as Wayne Prior noted, 'young but he was grown up already'.

Chappell had no problem with cockiness.

'You like to see a cricketer with some confidence. I don't mind if they are a bit over confident because you can knock a bit of that out of them but you can never inject any in. Hookesy had about the right amount but he had respect with it and that was an important combination.'

The respect Hookes had was for what he called 'the ethos of South Australian cricket'. He saw a line from Vic Richardson and Don Bradman through to Les Favell and on to Ian Chappell.

'So there was no thought to not playing that way or not attempting to play that way. I guess, at times, as my career evolved, I probably should have been a little more circumspect in my own batting but I never changed my outlook on cricket,' Hookes had said.

Mike Coward remembered the boy who emerged from Adelaide's western suburbs with a shock of blond hair and a fat bat. It simmered in 1975–76 and exploded the following season.

'It was pure excitement. He was uninhibited. His batting was a reflection of his personality and it was a joy to watch.'

In his second season for South Australia Hookes led all Sheffield Shield batsmen by averaging 79. In February 1977 his scores were 163 & 9 (against Victoria), 185 & 105 (against Queensland), and 35 & 156 (against New South Wales). The weight of runs saw him selected for Australia in the Centenary Test against England at the MCG in March. Wearing his old squash shoes, and with his bat taped up, he blasted five consecutive fours off English skipper Tony Greig. Gary Cosier (who was best man at Hookes's wedding) was watching from the player's rooms.

'The boys in the rooms were saying "Righto, righto, settle down." I said, "No chance of that, he will keep hitting them." And that is how he played – aggressive in the field. And [he was] very close to Ian. They liked each other and they batted a lot like each other.'

Those brash boundaries on the biggest stage were one of the memories that came from the crowd of mourners who waited in line to get into the ground for the memorial. A man in his twenties said: 'My dad's all-time best memory is the Centenary Test, [Hookes] hitting Tony Greig. [Now] every time Tony Greig says [on television] something my dad hates he says, "Yeah, well I remember when Hookesy smacked you around."'

Normally asking people to speak on television at a sensitive moment such as this is difficult, but without ever having to ask more than 'Do you have a memory of David Hookes?' people respectfully articulated what he meant to them.

A middle-aged woman held up a cutting from a suburban newspaper and said, 'This was taken up at Gawler Foodland where a lot of us went up there to meet him. Of course he was a very nice man, very pleasant, and that is my very good memory of David Hookes.'

One man said that once you made friends with Hookesy he was a friend for life, while another recounted how he watched him score the fastest first-class ton (off 34 balls) because he had 'got the shits with the Vics'.

Recollections of his deeds included his blue with New South

Wales captain Geoff Lawson after Hookes felt he had reneged on a gentleman's declaration agreement. Then there was his cunning plan that undid Dean Jones in a match against Victoria at the Adelaide Oval.

'Hookesy had a word with the bowler Andrew Zesers that Jones was standing out of his crease,' explained a middle-aged man is a whispered tone, as if he was worried someone might overhear.

'Next over, about third ball, he bowls this thing wide and it goes to Hookesy who has moved across from first slip. Jones of course is out of his crease and doesn't realise what is going on and Hookesy throws down the stumps. That was genius.'

By the end of his career Hookes had scored more runs for South Australia (9364) than Bradman, Chappell, Favell, Ridings and Richardson. After its 1975–76 Shield win, South Australia next won the competition in 1981–82, when Hookes was the captain.

It was estimated that ten thousand people turned up to mourn David Hookes at his Adelaide Oval memorial 22 years later.

*

Prior to the 1977 Centenary Test, the match in which Hookes took the long handle to the captain of England, the greatest ever collection of English and Australian Test cricketers gathered in Melbourne for a series of functions. Every past and present Australian and English player was invited and the functions saw

Don Bradman with Harold Larwood, Keith Miller with Denis Compton, and Ted Dexter with Bill Lawry.

When it came time for the match, the two teams lined up on the field to welcome, in order of seniority, captains of the past. Australia was led by 87-year-old Jack Ryder, still striding through the gate just weeks before he died. Following him was Bradman, Lindsay Hassett, Arthur Morris, Richie Benaud, Bob Simpson, Lawry and then Chappell. As he neared the gate Lawry heard a woman inside the fence say 'We love you, Bill'. Moments later she hissed, 'You're a mongrel, Chappell.'

Amid the suits and ties, Chappell strode out in a pale green safari suit, open-neck shirt and sunglasses. His fashion may have stood him apart but his true rebellion was taking place behind the scenes. After his blow up with the South Australian selectors a year earlier, Chappell had said he was through talking and it was time for action, but no-one would have predicted what was on the horizon. With the financial backing of Kerry Packer (who had bid unsuccessfully for the rights to televise Test cricket in Australia) Chappell helped arrange for 55 of the world's best cricketers to leave the establishment and play in a private exhibition competition called World Series Cricket (WSC).

World Series Cricket would market the game as never before and feed the appetite for one-day cricket. The ingredients were aggressive batting, fast bowling and brilliant fielding. Players wore coloured uniforms, played at night with a white ball and, most importantly for Chappell, were consulted, listened to and handsomely rewarded. He formalised a players' association to look after their interests. Packer paid for the legal fees to set it up and then the players reimbursed him.

The breakaway competition gutted traditional cricket, robbing it of its stars, the gate and sponsorship revenue. For two summers Australia had two teams, two competitions and two captains. Popular opinion was with the rebels and by the second season the financial bleeding was such that the establishment begged Packer for a merger. Ian Chappell captained Australia in WSC but it was Greg who returned to captain Australia after the merger. Ian played one more summer and left the field for the commentary box.

Hookes was an important signing for WSC because he was the poster boy of Australian cricket and represented the future. He risked his fledgling Test career to follow Chappell and he wasn't alone. Wayne Prior, Dennis Yagmich and Trevor Chappell also signed up but played mostly in the Cavaliers side. This was a WSC XI made up of reserve players that played regularly against the three main teams (Australia, the West Indies and the World) in country venues.

Prior bowled well but could never get into the first XI. He thought that while he was as quick as Lillee and Thomson his pace dropped off after several overs whereas the others could keep going. He used the money to buy a property in the Adelaide Hills and retired from cricket in 1985. He is still working, helping with the vintage at Yalumba Winery in the Barossa Valley.

Yagmich says one of the greatest innings he ever saw was Trevor Chappell making 56 for WSC Australia on a dodgy wicket at Lismore against the WSC World XI. He will never forget how he stood up to Michael Holding and Wayne Daniel as they worked him over. In the showers he was a mess of purple and yellow bruises from his knees to his shoulders. Trevor Chappell won Sheffield Shields while playing for both Western Australia and New South Wales. After WSC he played three Test matches for Australia, finally getting to wear his own baggy green cap and jumper.

Yagmich joined WSC after feeling his chances were limited in the establishment. He was dropped from the South Australian side early in the 1976–77 season without an obvious replacement. He rang Chappell who reportedly had turned down offers from New South Wales and Victoria and was commuting on weekends to captain–coach North Melbourne. Yagmich asked if he thought he should be dropped because, 'If he said I should have been then that would have been good enough for me' but Chappell could find no reason. Yagmich believed the rebellion the previous season was working against him. After WSC he returned to Western Australia where he grows wine grapes in the Swan Valley. Every year he returns to the Adelaide Oval for the Test match and to see old friends.

Yagmich wasn't the only one who felt the selectors soured on him. Rodney Hogg couldn't get a game for South Australia the next season. In 1977–78 he found longer spikes for his boots and with them the grip he needed for his front foot. His pace improved and on 1 December 1978 he opened the bowling for Australia against England at the Gabba. He picked up both openers – Graham Gooch and Geoff Boycott – in a six-wicket, first innings haul. He played 38 Test matches (claiming 123 wickets) and 71 one-day internationals (85 wickets).

His childhood friend from Northcote Gary Cosier played 18 Test matches and nine one-day internationals. His second and final century was a brilliant 168 against Pakistan at the MCG in January 1977. On the 1977 Ashes tour he took 5/18 against England in a one-day game at Edgbaston. That season he left South Australia for Queensland on a lucrative deal that still failed to win the state the Sheffield Shield. His back injury never allowed him to train easily and, after a final fling with Victoria, he retired in 1981. After a stint in sports management, including three years in Tangier, he returned to Queensland and works in sports psychology.

Rick Darling was water skiing on the River Murray when the call came that he had been selected for Australia. It meant he had fulfilled the family ambition to play for his country like his ancestor, Joe Darling. In January 1978 he made 65 on debut against India on the Adelaide Oval. He played 14 Test matches and 18 one-day internationals – the most memorable of which was when he shared a 60-run partnership with his childhood idol Doug Walters at the SCG. They were two country blokes doing the business in the big city.

The South Australian openers Rick Drewer and Ashley Woodcock both had long careers in private schools as physical education teachers and sports masters. Woodcock is batting coach at Kensington Cricket Club and Drewer remains a thorn in the side of the SACA with his regular letters to the editor and on-line opinions. He still loves music and has a sublime record collection.

Barry 'Nugget' Rees continues as a talisman for South Australian and Australian sides. In 2016 the home changing rooms at the Adelaide Oval were named in his honour.

Jeff Hammond's back healed enough for him to return to the state side in 1976–77 but it was as an opening batsman and not a strike bowler. His heroic work in the West Indies in 1973 would remain his only national duty. He retired in 1981 and coached South Australia to the Sheffield Shield title in 1995–96. He lives on a yacht that slowly makes its way around the island continent.

Bob Blewett's late first-class career started awkwardly but gathered momentum and he became a regular over the next three seasons. Three games into 1976–77 he took over as captain from Woodcock and so ended his career having been in charge of 21 of 25 matches he played. In January 1995 he was at the Adelaide Oval again to watch his son Greg score an unbeaten 102 against England in his Test debut.

For Barry Curtin, cricket died on the Adelaide Oval against India in November 1977. He was lbw to Erapalli Prasanna for a duck, but that wasn't it. He found his heart was no longer in it . Without Chappell the game seemed to lack its dynamic force.

'I was only 28 but the year after Ian went, Cose had gone, TJ and Rowdy retired. They were my core friends from the team. I was playing India on a beautiful day, it was an international game and I was at short cover. I can't explain why but I had a serious feeling that I don't want to be here anymore.'

He accepted an offer to play as a professional in England and stayed a few years. His love for Port Adelaide remains undiminished and he works for the football club running functions and hosting events. He hasn't had a drink for 25 years.

Geoff Attenborough ended his career in 1981 with 193 first-class wickets. His back was hurting and his young son was starting to ask why Dad was always away. He had stopped working as a butcher to run a sports store with his brother and later they moved into wholesale sporting goods. Another business venture in embroidery and printing saw his company take on uniform work for Cricket Australia. It has allowed for a comfortable retirement, which includes golf at Glenelg and being a bowling coach at Adelaide Cricket Club.

Despite announcing his imminent retirement in 1975, Ashley Mallett continued playing until 1981. By then he had played 38 Test matches, taking 132 wickets. The season after the strike, one of his desires was fulfilled when the SACA established a players' benefit fund. In Shield matches he collected 344 scalps, second only to Clarrie Grimmett with 513. After he finished playing he continued working as a journalist and author. Among his works are biographies of Grimmett, Walters, Thomson, Ian Chappell and Nugget Rees.

Mallett's old spin mate Terry Jenner retired after only one game in 1976–77. It was a thrashing by nine wickets at the hands of Western Australia. Jenner was in strife with the new SACA disciplinary tribunal. It had been formed during the winter due to the increasing reports being made by umpires from all grades. He was given a severe reprimand for his behaviour in a grade cricket match. He was finished.

The sour exit from the game he loved preceded the downward spiral that led to prison. It was cricket that raised him up again. Upon his release Rod Marsh asked him to come down to the Australian Cricket Academy, which was then based in Adelaide, and help out a young Victorian leggie – Shane Warne. Jenner's confidence and self-esteem were non-existent but Marsh saw a natural teacher in him emerge. Jenner and Warne recognised pieces of themselves in each other that were far beyond flippers and wrong 'uns.

As Warne became Australia's greatest bowler, Jenner became sought after as a coach, and he ended up with clients all over the world. The ABC used him as a radio commentator for the Adelaide Test and his insights into the game were valued by listeners. His natural storytelling and wit made him popular as an after-dinner speaker, and he released a biography. Friends and former team mates noted that this was a humbler version of TJ from the man they had played with. He called on them for an annual breakfast he hosted prior to the Adelaide Test to raise money for the Adelaide Central Mission, which had cared for his wife while he was incarcerated.

In April 2010 he suffered a severe heart attack while in England on a coaching trip. He survived the episode with only 15 per cent of his heart functioning. He was flown home where, six months later, a fundraiser was hosted by Chappell, with help from Warne and Walters to help pay his medical bills. TJ died at home in May 2011. He was 66 and knew the end was coming and that his memorial service would be held at the Adelaide Oval to which he said, 'I am flattered because it is a great honour. I don't think I deserve it.'

*

For Ian Chappell, how does winning the Sheffield Shield rank in his storied career?

'It was captaincy satisfaction as much as anything. I had a lot of satisfaction as a player in my career but that was not a leadership satisfaction. If the guys say, 40 years on, that I showed them how to win, to me that caps it off.

'One of the joys in life – not just cricket – is acquiring knowledge. Possibly more enjoyable than that is passing it on, and to see guys like Darling and Hookesy really blossom in that atmosphere. The going got tough – obviously at the start of the season everyone thought "Oh, South Australia, they are no good" – and then when we started to win people started to sit up and take notice so it got tougher but we still kept winning.

'I knew what TJ, Rowdy and Splinter would do, but to see the young guys blossom in that atmosphere was really satisfying. It is probably the thing I am most proud of as a captain – that we went from last to first and won the Shield.'

As is so often the case in Chapelliland, he provides a sting in the tale.

'That statement I made after the Victoria game, that I wasn't playing for the SACA anymore and that I was just playing for the team …' he says, pausing for effect. 'Apparently that really got up the administrator's noses.'

'So I am really glad I made it.'

ACKNOWLEDGMENTS & SOURCES

This book was written using an amalgam of sources, primarily interviews conducted with the players from 1975–76, with secondary information from the work of others. I am grateful to the players, all of whom enthusiastically agreed to reminisce and who endured follow-up calls and emails to confirm details.

Over the years, through my work as a journalist, I have interviewed Ian Chappell, Ashley Mallett, Terry Jenner and David Hookes for various reasons. If I might offer one piece of advice to young reporters it is always keep your notes. Those interview transcripts were invaluable, particularly with Hookes and Jenner.

As a young reporter working for Channel Nine I recall the brash Hookes striding through the newsroom for a meeting with the hierarchy. As he left he wandered past my desk and introduced himself. He never forgot my name and it was a mark of his character that whatever the circumstances (and there were a few hairy ones) he always took a call and gave considered answers.

He rang one day to suggest getting a camera down to state training because 'you will want some shots of this stocky teenage left-hander from Salisbury who is going to play for Australia'. That first vision of Darren Lehmann hopefully still lives somewhere in an archive. Through Lehmann, I like to think the spirit of Richardson, Bradman, Favell, Chappell, and Hookes continues to be imparted to the Australian XI.

The biographies and memoirs of Hookes, Jenner, Mallett and Chappell were all helpful, as was Frank Tyson's *The Hapless Hookers* – the only account of the summer of 1975–76. Mike Coward who covered the remarkable season wrote the beautiful coffee table book *The Chappell Years*, and some of his interviews for the accompanying ABC television series *Cricket in the 70s*, produced by Lincoln Tyner, gave insights into the era and its players. Coward's conduct and language, along with that of contemporaries Alan Shiell and Gordon Schwartz, remains a high-water mark for sports journalism in South Australia.

Many people helped with information, contacts and as sounding boards. Thanks to Denis Brien, Bernard Whimpress, Lawrie Colliver, Barry Nicholls, Geoff Hutchison, Liz March, Daniel Keane and John Harms.

I am grateful to Martin Hughes and Keiran Rogers at Affirm Press who took on the idea and backed it enthusiastically and professionally, and to Paul Connolly for tidying and improving the manuscript.